W9-BGM-831

GO organize!

CONQUER CLUTTER IN 3 SIMPLE STEPS

GO organize!

CONQUER CLUTTER IN 3 SIMPLE STEPS

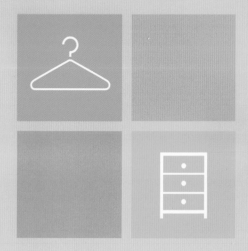

MARILYN BOHN

BETTERWAY HOME
CINCINNATI, OHIO

Other fine Betterway Home Books are available from your local bookstore, or home improvement store or direct from the publisher. Visit our Web site at www.fwmedia.com.

13 12 11 10 09   5 4 3 2 1

Distributed in Canada by Fraser Direct, 100 Armstrong Avenue, Georgetown, Ontario,
    Canada L7G 5S4, Tel: (905) 877-4411
Distributed in the U.K. and Europe by David & Charles, Brunel House, Newton Abbot,
    Devon, TQ12 4PU, England, Tel: (+44) 1626 323200, Fax: (+44) 1626 323319, E-mail:
    postmaster@davidandcharles.co.uk
Distributed in Australia by Capricorn Link, P.O. Box 704, S. Windsor NSW, 2756 Australia,
    Tel: (02) 4577-3555

Library of Congress Cataloging in Publication Data
Bohn, Marilyn,
    Go organize! : conquer clutter in 3 simple steps / by Marilyn Bohn. -- 1st ed.
        p. cm.
    Includes index.
    ISBN 978-1-55870-889-1 (alk. paper)
    1. Storage in the home. 2. House cleaning. 3. Orderliness. I. Title.
    TX309.B655 2009
    648'.8--dc22
                                2009020935

Edited by Jacqueline Musser; Designed by Clare Finney; Production coordinated by Mark Griffin; Photographs on pages 2, 104, 124, 176, 198 and 208 by Ric Deliantoni

ABOUT THE AUTHOR

Marilyn Bohn is an organizing expert and author. She is also the founder of Get It Together Organizing. She has been featured on KSL Television, KSL Newsradio, and KLBC Radio and has taught multiple organizing classes within her community. Her articles have appeared in local and national newspapers and company newsletters. Marilyn's focus is to help people reduce clutter in their homes, offices, and lives. In addition to face-to-face organizing assistance, Marilyn also offers convenient virtual online organizing via her Web site, www.marilynbohn.com.

Before becoming a professional organizer, she worked in the social service field as a child protection worker and a contract analyst. She is a member of the National Association of Professional Organizers.

Visit her Web site to sign up for free organizing tips, and visit her online store for organizing kits, Game Savers ™ and organizing supplies.

ACKNOWLEDGMENTS

A special thank you to Cindy, my daughter and business manager, who was the catalyst encouraging me to follow my passion to help others organize. Thank you to Edna Hess, Kim Condrin of Organize to Order, and to Shahar and Nashlah Boyayan of BuzzBooster.

Thank you to my daughters who constantly support and encourage me in everything I chose to pursue. A special thanks to Julie who helped me with my first outline and to Janice who inspired me with editing and proofreading every chapter.

Many thanks to my friends for the support they gave me as I wrote this book, and to Jackie, my editor at Betterway Home, who is a pleasure to work with and was very helpful in guiding me through this experience.

To my daughters Cindy, Debbie, Julie, and Janice
for all their help in writing this book.

Contents

Introduction   10

1.   Lights On Organizing System   12

2.   Getting Started   28

3.   Entryways   42

4.   The Living Room   54

5.   The Kitchen   66

6.   The Master Bedroom   88

7.   Children's Bedrooms   104

8.   Linen Closets   124

9.   The Bathroom   132

10.   The Family Room   144

11. Home Office and Paperwork   158

12. The Craft Room or Area   176

13. The Laundry Room   188

14. Downsizing   198

15. Memorabilia and Inherited Items   208

16. The Storage Room   216

17. Live It, Love It, Lights On   224

Appendices

   Searchlight Worksheet   231

   Spotlight Worksheet   233

Index   236

Introduction

I wrote this book as a friend. My intention is to encourage you each step of the way in your organizing journey. This book is for those who want to be organized, and for those who want to be more organized.

Everyone I know and have worked with wants to be organized. When people don't live up to what they think "being organized" means, they can become discouraged and depressed. Being organized means something different to everyone. There is no right or wrong way to be organized. What counts is that it works for you.

People I work with often feel embarrassed because their homes and offices are cluttered and disorganized. But, you know, it is nothing to feel embarrassed or bad about! Being organized is a skill that can be learned. No one is disorganized because they want to be. Many people have busy schedules and can feel overwhelmed by all there is to do, constantly being bombarded with different projects, errands, and "to do" lists. I have never met anyone who needs help organizing because they are lazy.

Go Organize! helps you conquer clutter in three simple steps. In it, I will guide you through the entire organizing process using my Lights On Organizing System. You'll learn how to use the Searchlight, Spotlight, and Green Light to transform your surroundings and increase the wattage in your home. Each chapter has been developed to specifically help you organize your kitchen, bedroom, closet, home office, storage areas, and other rooms in your home. You'll also find useful advice on organizing inherited items and memorabilia and learn how to downsize for a smaller living space. This book is filled with tips, stories, and creative ideas on how to organize.

1 Lights On Organizing System

Everything in our lives either moves us toward our goals or farther away from them. Do you feel it is time to start clearing out clutter so you can move toward a better, peaceful, brighter, and happier life? Do you want to spend more time doing more of the things you like to do? The Lights On Organizing System will help you reach these goals.

Lights On Organizing is a powerful, electrifying, and simple three-step process to getting and staying organized. It is measured on a wattage scale of 1 to 10. A 1 is the lowest wattage where your energy is low. It is like living in a dim, dark environment. Feelings of depression, anger, frustration, and dissatisfaction happen at this low wattage. A 10 is the highest wattage where the feeling is one of light, brightness, and increased energy. It feels peaceful, happy, relaxed, and welcoming.

There are three simple steps to Lights On Organizing:

Step 1 is Searchlight. The Searchlight is the process of evaluating what your home currently looks like and feels like to you. Also, take a look at how you are using the space in your home. It is a process of identifying problems and determining both what is and is not working. The benefits of using the Searchlight step is that you will assess and determine the problem areas in your home and the places you want to declutter so you can reclaim your home and your life. As you walk through your house, check where you are on the wattage scale in the sidebar on page 15.

To live in a light environment, your life needs to reflect at a high wattage, which is Lights On.

Step 2 is Spotlight. After identifying the problem areas, this is the step where you write your goals, create your vision and develop a plan. This process will be a snap by using the goal-setting worksheet found on pages 233–235. Setting goals that can be broken down into easy and manageable steps gives you direction, courage, an I-can–do-this attitude, and peace of mind.

Step 3 is Green Light. This is where the rubber meets the road and changes are made. You roll up your sleeves and get down to work following easy-to-understand instructions. I will help you every step of the way. You will learn all you need to know to be organized, but more than that, you will be able to take action.

We will be using these three steps in every room. I will be with you all the way, explaining and showing you how to reach your goals. You'll also find Paula's Stories throughout the book. Her stories illustrate real-life situations. She uses the Searchlight to evaluate the rooms in her home, the Spotlight to set goals, and the Green Light to make changes. My hope is that you can relate to Paula's experiences as you read her stories. Her stories are designed to show you how to use the Lights On Organizing System in a real-life setting. Let's explore the Lights On Organizing System a little more.

Wattage Scale

1–2	*Lights are very dim and dark.* You dread going into the room. The space makes you depressed and unhappy. You have no idea where to start or what to do to improve the situation. It takes you several minutes to find anything you're looking for. You are surrounded by things that drain you, either the objects themselves or entire rooms. Things are dirty and in disrepair.
3–4	*Lights are dim.* You feel unmotivated and overwhelmed at this wattage. There is a lot of "stuff" in the room but none of it has a home, and you have no connection to the items. Your "stuff" has turned into junk. You are drained by your possessions.
5–6	*Lights are neutral.* You don't have a strong negative or a strong positive reaction. The area is OK but nothing more. Everything is functional for the most part, but nothing in the room excites you. You aren't drained by your surroundings, yet they bring you little to no enjoyment.
7–8	*Lights are bright.* Life is good. You feel happy each time you use or look at your things. You know where things are and are surrounded by what you like and use.
9–10	*Lights are radiant.* You love each room and everything in the rooms. You feel great, and your surroundings bring you joy. You know where everything is. You have surrounded yourself with what you love. Your surroundings give you energy. You are organized and often do maintenance, which allows you to keep organized. You don't collect junk and are very choosy about what you allow in your life and home.

SEARCHLIGHT

Before we can increase the wattage in our homes and make positive changes, we need to find out what changes are needed. Use your mind, eyes, and heart as a "searchlight." Take the time to search the rooms and spaces in your home and see what needs to change. This is the time when you honestly assess the condition of your home and identify the problem areas that you want to change and organize. If you need some fortification as you start, grab a treat and a drink (I'm thinking of chocolate and water, not a margarita).

> Part of organizing is figuring out what works and what doesn't work.

Start with the positives. Look for what is working and for things that light you up. You will find there is a lot that is already working for you. Be objective. I know emotions can get in the way of making an honest assessment. Don't beat yourself up! This is the time to think about how you want things to function and to look as well as about what changes are needed.

After you've listed the positive things that are working, honestly assess the things that aren't working. This handy list will help you in the Searchlight step:

1. Choose a room to organize.
2. Choose a place in that room and start your search from the inside out—meaning start with closets, drawers, or cupboards before you evaluate open spaces.
3. Identify needs by asking yourself these questions:
   a. Is the space orderly?
   b. Are there things here you can you get rid of?
   c. Is it easy for you to find everything, or do you waste a lot of time looking for things?
   d. Does everything have a home? (Are things contained or scattered around?)

Paula's Searchlight Experience

Paula was at her wits end. She felt she lived her life in crisis mode because her home and her life were so disorganized. She was frequently late and often lost important papers. Everywhere she looked, there was clutter. She wasn't happy, and her family wasn't happy either. When she decided to try the Light's On Organizing System, she used the Searchlight and realized her home left her feeling a 2 on the wattage scale. She felt most drained in her bedroom. Working from the inside out, she started evaluating the room by opening her closet. When she opened the closet door, she immediately felt overwhelmed. Shoes were strewn all over the floor along with clothes, belts, and other odds and ends. The wire hangers were sagging and clothes were falling off the hangers. The built-in shelves looked like a tornado had hit; everything was so jumbled. She had no idea what was in the boxes on the shelves. She rated this area a 2 on the wattage scale. There were boxes and built-in shelves, but she wasn't using them in a way that worked for her. She took a picture of the closet and then wrote down what she needed to change: She needed to get the clothes, belts, purses, and accessories off the closet floor; she needed to get new hangers that would properly protect her clothes and keep them from falling; she needed to know what was in each box in the closet; she needed to use the shelf space better so she could store everything she needed to in her closet; she needed to have a plan to organize her shoes so she could find them easily; she needed to get rid of items she no longer wore. Paula felt better after she made her list. She knew there was still a lot of work to be done, but honestly evaluating the closet and knowing what she needed to change filled her with hope.

e. Do you keep only things you use?

f. Does each item light you up on a scale of 7 or above?

g. Does this space help you make the best use of your time?

h. Do you feel like you can't find anything you like or enjoy in your home even though you are surrounded by things?

i. Do you dread doing housework or put it off indefinitely because of all the clutter?

4. Rate your wattage (use the wattage scale on page 15). How do you feel about that particular space in the room? If you don't feel good about it, you are right where you need to be.

5. Based on your assessment, make a list of the things you need to change in this room. Be sure to write these down. If you have a camera, take a picture in each room. (This is something many professional organizers do.) Later, after you finish organizing the space, take another picture. It is fun and rewarding to look back and see the progress you made and see how great everything looks. (Yes, your house will look great!) When things are organized, we forget how they used to look. It is a great visual reminder to compare before and after photos. If you don't have a camera, don't let this stop you from making your list.

The Searchlight checklist is to be used in each room. Don't worry. We'll walk through this process together for every room in your home in the following chapters. The Searchlight worksheet on pages 231–232 will also help you with this important first step. Once your problem areas have been identified, you are ready for the second step in the Lights On Organizing System.

> If you were talking to your friend about her home the way you are talking to yourself about your home, how long would she be your friend?

Paula's Spotlight Experience

Let's revisit Paula as she starts the Spotlight process in her bedroom closet. Paula thought about what kind of closet would increase her wattage to a 10. She pictured her shoes neatly organized on the closet floor; a separate box each for belts, scarves, and purses and each box neatly sitting on a shelf; she pictured only clothes she liked to wear hanging on the rod so she could easily put clothes away and find clothes to wear. She wrote this "big picture" vision down and then started breaking down the vision into steps she could take: She would buy a shoe organizing system and use it, donating or throwing away old shoes that she doesn't wear. She would make sure she had containers large enough to hold her belts, purses, and scarves, and she would label each container. She would sort through each clothing item in her closet and donate clothes that don't fit or don't make her feel good. She would then move all out-of-season clothes into storage containers that she could fit under her bed. She would arrange all her clothes by category (blouses, skirts, pants, etc.). She would replace her wire hangers with wooden or padded hangers that would better support her clothing. Paula felt great about her new goals and couldn't wait to get started. She had a lot of clothing in her closet. She decided to break the closet down into zones (e.g., the floor, the closet rod, top shelf and the cube shelves) and organize one zone each week until it was done. She set a target date to have it completed and wrote it on her calendar.

> Break your "big picture" vision down into smaller steps you can take.

SPOTLIGHT

After you use the Searchlight to identify the problem areas you want to change, move on to the second step of the Lights On Organizing System, the Spotlight. A Spotlight is a powerful stage light controlled by a person. The light is used to focus intensely on specific areas. In the Spotlight step, you focus on the problem areas and create a plan for changing them. You will set goals, create your vision, and develop a plan with the help of the Spotlight worksheet on pages 233–235.

There are three steps to successful goal setting:

1. Create the "big picture" of what you want.
2. Break this vision down into smaller pieces that can be achieved one step at a time.
3. Decide when you are going to reach this goal by setting a deadline. This gives you a specific date to work towards.

GREEN LIGHT

Once you search out problem areas and set goals for organizing those areas, you've got the Green Light to take action: Proceed, move ahead, take your foot off the brake, and begin. Go, go, go! Here are some things that will make the work of organizing easier:

Containers

Don't rush out and buy all new containers. First, find out if you have containers that you can use in your home. There are many things that can be recycled and reused as containers: shoe boxes, cereal boxes, plastic fruit containers, baby food jars, checkbook boxes, glass mugs, baskets, and large packaging boxes, just to name a few. You can paint or decorate these reused containers to make them more fun and appealing.

Baskets are great containers that help cut clutter in three ways: First, things

Choosing the Right Container

When Sherry's daughters were young, they had a drawer where they kept their crayons and colored pencils, but the crayons and colored pencils were scattered throughout the drawer. She decided to buy a container for them. Sherry sorted the crayons and pencils and placed them in the container. She was so proud as she didn't usually use containers. The next morning the crayons and pencils were dumped out of the box. It had become a trough for the toy horses. She tried to salvage the pencil box several times over the next few years only to find it serving as a cash register for her daughters' make-believe store, an altar piece for some tribal activity, dollhouse furniture, and a boat for dolls. The container was never used as a pencil box and the crayons and pencils were scattered all over in the drawer. Sherry concluded from this experience that containers didn't work.

If one type of container doesn't work as you intended, don't give up. Containers help you stay organized.

What she didn't realize is, she did have other options. She could have purchased other containers for her girls to use for their play, or she could have purchased a drawer divider rather than this type of container for the crayons and pencils. She could have labeled the container and explained to the girls what the container was to be used for. If one type of container doesn't work as you intended, don't give up. Containers are a marvelous way to organize and stay organized.

are contained without having to be folded perfectively (and who likes doing that all the time?); second, it limits the amount of things you can keep; and third, they are attractive so they can be left out in a room rather than hidden in cupboards or drawers.

Tip: If you do buy organizing supplies, such as containers, save your receipts in case you need to return them. It will save you time and hassle when returning. Place an envelope in your planner or purse to keep receipts in.

Organizing Tool Kit

Having a kit you can move from room to room will save you time. Essentials in the kit are a timer with the hour and minute features; tape measure; wide, double-sided sticky tape; cleaning cloth and cleaning spray; notepad and pen; hammer and screwdriver.

Timer: When you start to work on a room, area, or project, set a timer. A timer lets you focus on the task at hand without being distracted by the clock. When the timer goes off, you're finished for that session, unless you are in a good rhythm. In that case set the timer for more time. Also, use it when you take breaks to remind you to come back to the project.

Tape measure: This is to measure the size of your containers and the space where you plan to use them. It can also be used to measure the size of what you are going to store (height and width) so you can purchase the correct size of container.

Wide, double-sided sticky tape: Use this under containers in any drawer to keep them from sliding back and forth.

Cleaning Cloth and Cleaning Spray: As you clear off shelves and flat surfaces, give the surfaces a good cleaning while they are empty. You'll have a fresh start when you place items back on them.

Notepad and Pen: Use these to jot down notes as you go—things you need to buy, measurements you have taken—and record what works for you and what doesn't work for you in each room.

Hammer and Screwdriver: These are to hang pictures and for lots of other uses. If you share tools with someone else in the house, I suggest you don't share the items in your organizing tool kit or they may get lost.

Work From the Inside Out

When you start working in a room, work from the inside out! This means if there is a closet or drawer, start there first. Why? There are two primary reasons:

1. There are always things out in the room that need to be put away into a drawer, bookcase, cupboard, or closet. If you start organizing the open areas of the room before organizing the closet, drawers and shelves, you are wasting time. It is a waste of time to put items into a closet or drawer because when you start organizing that space, you will just have to take them back out again.
2. You will always create space that you can use for other items.

Save yourself time and energy, work from the inside to the outside.

Set Time Limits

Remember to use the trusty timer in your tool kit. When starting a project (be it a full room, a closet or a drawer), there are two ways to do it:

1. If you are dreading the task with much trepidation, set your timer for twenty minutes to one hour. When it goes off, *stop*, unless you are in a great rhythm and you know you won't get burned out by working for a longer period of time. I don't want you to work until you get burned out. Set your timer the second time for twenty minutes and see how you are feeling at the end of this time period. You can work for longer periods of time, but don't work so long at one time that you don't ever want to return.
2. Start working and keep on working until the task is done. You know yourself, and you know if this will work for you.

Just by knowing you have a set time limit can make a difference mentally and physically.

Categorize Your Spaces

As you organize in a room, categorize all of the spaces in it, including closets, drawers, shelves, and open spaces. There are four categories for space:

1. *Premium Spaces:* This is the space that is at your eye level and just above, reaching down to about waist level. It is "right in your face" and is the easiest and most convenient to use. You don't need to bend or stretch to reach this space. This is the area you get in and out of on a daily basis. Use this only for those things you use regularly.
2. *Secondary Spaces:* Items placed here are those used about once a week—things like table linens, extra food items, fine china, or sheets (if not stored in a linen closet).
3. *Semi-Storage:* These are items that are used once a year, such as holiday items, seasonal dishes, seasonal clothes, and camping gear. Store these

Time Limits Provide Motivation

I have a storage space under the stairs in my utility room. It needed organizing! I evaluated this space by using my Searchlight, and I rated myself and this area as a 1 on the wattage scale. I didn't even know what was in the space. Using the Spotlight, I set goals to add shelves and to arrange this area so it was useful. I would also write down in my notebook what I stored here.

When I started using the Green Light, I set my timer for one hour. I dreaded this project, but just by knowing I had given myself permission to only work for a set length of time gave me a whole different attitude. When the timer rang, I was surprised because it didn't feel like I had been working that long. I reset my timer and kept on working until I had reached all of my goals. Setting a time limit made all the difference in the world.

items where they can be accessed but aren't taking up valuable space within your home. These items can be kept in your attic or storage room, and then rotated in and out of your cupboards, closets, and living space as needed.

4. *Hard-Core Storage:* These are items placed in labeled plastic bins that "live" in your garage, shed, or storage room. These containers only need to be opened every few years. These boxes could contain yearbooks, childhood items, memorabilia you have inherited and are passing down to other generations, and items you are storing for your adult children who have moved out of your home.

Putting Things Away

Have you ever noticed that putting things away seems more difficult and time-consuming than getting them out? It might not be that it is hard; it could be that you need to learn different habits. How hard is it to hang up a blouse instead of tossing it on a chair, which will mean you have to spend more time putting it away later? When the closet is organized into categories and there is space to hang clothes, it is easier to put them away.

Every item needs a home—a permanent place where it is kept—to make it much easier to know where to return items after using them. When there is a place for everything you use and you know where to return things, it takes less time and actually is easier to put things away than to toss them somewhere to be dealt with later.

If towels are jumbled in the closet, you can pull one out with little effort, but putting them back in a neat stack is difficult if there isn't a place for them. This also is true for other items you use on a daily basis in every room in your home. Categorizing your spaces and making homes for everything will make it easier for you to put things away where they belong after they are used.

Make It Fun

Whatever it takes to have fun while clearing clutter and creating space—do it! Maybe it will be crossing off each step as you go, munching on a celery stick (make mine chocolate), listening to some favorite music, or rewarding yourself when you have finished with a new CD, fresh flowers, or a trip to the spa.

WRAP UP

Now you know the three steps to Lights On Organizing. First, you'll use the Searchlight and assess the organizing needs in your home. Fill out the Searchlight worksheet room by room to choose what is working and what is not working for you and identify what room you want to start in. Identifying the problem is a great start.

Second, with your Spotlight, focus on a plan to get organized. You know the wattage you feel in each room, and you know where you are headed to increase your wattage. Break your goals down into manageable steps and set deadlines for completing your goals.

Third, give yourself the Green Light to take action. Each chapter in this book explains step by step how to organize a different room, so pick your room and let's get going.

Getting Started

"Where do I start?" As a professional organizer I am often asked this question when I work in clients' homes. The answer is—it really doesn't matter. That's right. You can start wherever you would like, but I will give you specific instructions to help you decide what is best for you. What does matter is that you do start and stay with it until the area is organized and functions the way you want it to. You may be thinking: *That's easy for you to say; I've tried to get organized, and I just can't.* I have helped hundreds of women become organized, and I can help you be organized, too, by using these three simple steps: Searchlight, Spotlight, and Green Light.

Paula's Story

Have you ever had days like this? Paula decided she was going to organize her bedroom. She started right after her children left for school. In her bedroom, she found a baseball cap that needed to go to the hall closet; on her way to the closet she saw a broken figurine so she went to get the glue. She discovered there was no glue, so she headed down the hall to add it to her grocery list. As she passed her daughter's room, she noticed the bed was unmade. She thought, *Ah, I will make her bed*. As she was making the bed, she spied a book she had been looking for and was on her way to put it on the bookshelf when she realized she was getting tired and remembered she hadn't taken her vitamin pill, so off to the kitchen she went for the pill. There were dishes in the sink that would only take a few minutes to take care of, so she loaded them in the dishwasher. She tripped over shoes someone had kicked off in the hallway, and off to the person's room she headed with the shoes in hand. Her day went on and on like this until the next thing she knew, the kids were walking in the door from school, and nothing had been done toward organizing her bedroom.

It is not unusual to have days like Paula's (see the sidebar above) because, as busy women, we have busy lives. It doesn't matter if we are single, married, have children, have no children, work outside the home, are stay-at-home moms, or are empty nesters; we are all busy. There are tons of things we feel we need to get done every day. We all have good intentions, and we are doing the right things. But the feeling, and sometimes the reality, that we never get anything done leaves us frustrated, stressed out, and discouraged. We can overcome that discouragement and frustration by creating an organized plan and then committing the time, energy, and focus to carry out that plan. I'll teach you how to do just that (and avoid days like Paula's) in this chapter.

SEARCHLIGHT

Let's use the Lights On Organizing System to help you decide where to start organizing in your home. The first step is the Searchlight. Remember, the Searchlight lets you find what is and isn't working for you. Use the wattage chart (see page 15) to determine how lit up your home makes you feel. Go room by room writing down the wattage you currently feel in each space. This will help you decide where to start organizing. You can start with the area that needs the most work, or you can start with the room that needs the least work and build energy and confidence to tackle the harder spots. The choice is yours.

> It's not as important where you start, just that you start!

If you think your whole house needs organizing, I suggest one of two places to start: either the front entryway or your master bedroom. Next, the bathroom(s), followed by the kitchen, family room, children's rooms, laundry room, office, craft room, storage room, and finally the garage.

Why Start in the Front Entryway?

This area gives your guests and family their first impressions of your home. You want them to feel welcome. It is typically a smaller space, so it can be organized pretty quickly, and it will leave you feeling encouraged knowing you can accomplish your goal to be organized.

Why the Master Bedroom?

This is your very own personal sanctuary, a room you can walk into and feel peaceful and calm. It is a haven from the day's hectic schedule and activities. You can close the door and have a few minutes of quiet time during the day. It is the room to enjoy time alone with your significant other. You can read a good book or magazine as you snuggle down in bed or lounge in a comfy chair. It can be a place for quiet meditation. You could even call it your time-out room—maybe the kids will leave you alone.

What About the Storage Areas?

I have been asked "why not organize my storage room first?" You may feel this is the room that needs the most help so you want to tackle it right away. I suggest you leave that room to the last for several reasons. The rooms you live in are the most important rooms to organize first because you are in them every day. You want to surround yourself with light in your life. Storage rooms often become the dumping ground for everything you and your family don't know what to do with and for the things you don't have room for in your home. These cast-off items become jumbled up with items that actually belong in the storage area. It is too overwhelming to start here. As you use the Lights On Organizing System and learn how to use the Searchlight, Spotlight and Green Light, you will gain the skills and confidence to tackle your storage room.

> The rooms you actually live in are the most important rooms to organize first.

Tip: *If one room is driving you crazy and you just can't stop thinking about it (or avoiding it), then start in that room.*

SPOTLIGHT

With the Searchlight step, you checked out all the rooms in your home and you chose one room you want to start in. Now with your Spotlight we will set some goals. You may lament (with a tiny, nervous giggle) that your entire home needs organizing; rooms, closets, and cupboards. Great, this will be the overall goal—the "big picture." You are going to turn up the wattage in your home and "live light."

The Spotlight stage is where you make a plan that will give you both peace of mind and direction. Break it down into simple, manageable steps, such as these:

1. Decide how much time you can devote to the project. This is not something you will *find* time to do; it is something you want to *make* time to do.

2. Make an appointment with yourself to organize this room; write it down on your calendar or in your planner. Take it one step at a time. Set your timer for the length of time you plan on working. Start with twenty minutes to one hour. The more time you work, the more you will get done. But I don't want you to burn out by working too long or too fast. Don't walk faster than you can run!

3. Set a deadline for you to finish, and then work toward completing the project by that date.

Tip: When your goal is organizing your entire home and you have it broken down into manageable sections, you will need to commit to bigger chunks of time to accomplish your goal as you proceed. Once things are organized, a few minutes a week (and not necessarily all at the same time) will give you enough time to keep your home organized. Use pockets of time to organize (straighten things up and put things away)—minutes when you are waiting for someone or you don't feel like starting a big project but you have a few minutes you can use.

Slow and Steady Wins the Race

I bet you want everything organized right now, and you want it done and over with! I am the same way. In fact, I bought a sign that reads, *Enjoy the Journey*. I have the tendency to want the project to be finished so I can move on to something else, instead of enjoying the experience, or the journey. Give yourself permission to take small bites, start slowly, and pick up speed as you go. Keep in mind, it isn't a race. Personally, it is a big relief just to know that it is okay to go slow; not everything has to be done right now.

Eating an elephant is only possible one bite at a time. It's the same with organizing: Start slow and work steady, doing a little at a time. You will see big results that will last!

GREEN LIGHT

Let's get going in the room you chose to organize! This is the exciting part because in this step, you will see results, get rid of things you haven't known what to do with, create space, and have homes for things so you will be able to find them when you want them. Here are ideas and suggestions of literally where to begin within the room you have chosen to organize. Choose one of the following and begin.

- Remember to work from the inside out in every room. If there is a closet, start there. If there are drawers, start with the top drawer and work your way down to the bottom drawer.
- Organize surfaces second. After you have organized the internal parts of the room, if there is a flat surface (such as the top of dressers, tables, or counters), organize there.
- Next, either start with the most cluttered place or the least cluttered place. It is your decision. You are in control (even if you don't feel like you are). By doing the most cluttered first, the area won't hang over your head as you do the rest of the room. By organizing the least cluttered

space, you will see progress quicker. For example: You could organize an entire book case, which takes longer than just a magazine rack.

Eliminate Distractions

Remember Paula's story from the beginning of the chapter? She had the desire to organize, but she didn't get far because she got distracted. When she uses the principles of the Green Light, she will be able to stay focused and finish her work. Knowing where to start and how to approach the work will help you get started, and eliminating outside distractions will help you finish. I'll give you tips to help you stay in the Green Light to stay focused.

> Organizing is like climbing a mountain; standing on the top isn't the only reward. There are a lot of beautiful things to see on the climb to the top.

- Collect four containers. Before you begin any organizing project, be sure you have four essential containers with you: one for trash, one for recycling, one for items you plan to donate, and one for items that belong in another room. This last container is your "belongs elsewhere" (BE) basket. Put items that belong in other rooms in this basket and carry on with your organizing. Don't leave the room to put things away. If you find a broken item that you want to repair, place it in your BE basket and continue organizing. Don't stop your work to make the repair. Finish the task at hand first. You can deal with the items in your BE basket when you are finished organizing for the day. If other people live with you, distribute the items and let them help.
- Ignore the phone. When the phone rings (it will), let the answering machine pick it up. Have a planned time when you will listen to and return messages, say at 10 A.M., 1 P.M. and so forth. This will save you

a lot of time and you will quickly get more done! Let your family and friends know you will be returning calls at those times.

- Take your organizing tool kit (see page 22) with you.
- Use your timer. Take your timer in the room with you, and set it for the length of time you initially plan on working. If you have to leave for a break, take your timer with you and set it for five minutes to remind you what you are doing so you don't do what Paula did. Make it your goal to stay in the room for the entire designated time. Your energy will be focused and you'll make the most of your time.
- Take your drink and treats with you, that way you won't have to leave to get them.
- Wear clothes to get you in the mood to organize—comfortable, every-day clothes.
- Use a slow cooker to make dinner, or order out so you don't have to think about fixing dinner. This will help you to stay focused.
- Tell someone else what your plans are and then report back to her with your success. You will also get encouragement from her.
- Keep your written goals with you and cross them off as you complete each one.
- Get up one hour earlier or work after the kids are in bed to eliminate distractions.

INCREASE YOUR WATTAGE

As you organize, you'll find you need to make lots of decisions. Here are some guidelines to help you make the brightest choices based on your situation.

To Keep or Not to Keep, That Is the Question

Keep only the things you love, things that light you up, things that you use and enrich your life. As you look at an item, trying to decide if you are keeping it or getting rid of it, give it a rating from 1 watt to 10 watts on the wattage scale (see page 15); 1 watt is low voltage; 10 watts is high voltage. If you give an object a wattage of 7 or above, it is a keeper. If it is at 4 watts or below, let it go. Ask yourself questions like: Do I love this or do I just like it? Do I like it enough to keep it? Can I live without it? Will I miss it if I don't have it? Will someone else love it or get more use out of it than I do? Is the space it takes up worth it to me? How does it make me feel? Am I lit up about it? Am I keeping this out of guilt? Am I keeping this out of fear? What is the worst thing that would happen if this item was removed from my life? What is the best thing that would happen if this item was removed from my life?

> Let go to lighten up.

When you are living in an environment where you are surrounded with the wattage of 4 or below, your energy is being drained, and you are living in a dark space, even if you aren't consciously aware of it. If your home and possessions all reflect a wattage of 7 or above, you are living in a bright environment. This is a place where you are lit up, happy, peaceful, and have positive space around you, which also reflects in your life. If you are living in the neutral zone of 5 to 6, you are not being drained, but I encourage you to turn up the wattage to a 7 or above. You'll enjoy your surroundings even more.

Only keep things you have a use for. If you are using it now or have used it in the last year, then it is a keeper. The exception to this rule is don't keep useful things that have bad memories attached to them. Maybe someone you don't care for gave you the object or you bought it and you wish you had returned it but never did.

Keep only a selection of memorabilia you have inherited. You don't have to keep everything. What was important to someone else will not necessarily be important to you. Donate items to enrich and bless someone else's life, and you'll find you are blessed as well; you won't be dealing with clutter. If you're still not sure about donating something, but you know you'll never use the item and really don't

You Don't Have to Keep Everything

When Diane lived in the dorms at the local university, her roommate, Tina, moved out but left her iron in the room. Diane had no way of contacting Tina so she kept the iron. For years, whenever Diane used the iron, even though it was infrequent, it brought back negative emotions because Tina had been a horrible roommate. Diane put the Lights On Organizing System to the test, and she donated the iron and bought a new one. Her new, upscale iron lights her up every time she uses it. She feels good and it doesn't trigger a negative memory of Tina when she uses her iron.

Angela had a high-end, free-standing mixer. She wanted to sell it because she never used it, and it just took up space on her kitchen counter. She kept it for years because everyone told her she should keep it because it was a great machine. One day, as she was organizing her kitchen, she realized it didn't matter what other people said about the mixer, she never used it, she didn't want it, and it took up valuable counter space. She sold the machine, and she's never regretted it.

Remember, it's your home and your possessions; make it work for you. If you want to sell or donate your belongings to make more space in your house, it's OK. Don't let other people's expectations keep you from achieving your organization goals.

> It's your home and possessions. Don't let other people's expectations keep you from achieving your organization goals.

want it, you can take a photo and then donate the item. Keep the photo on your computer or develop it and put it in a book. You'll keep the memory of the object without having the clutter.

My daughter made two salt dough dolls when she was four years old. I thought they were the cutest things, and I was sure she would always want them. They were funny looking and splashed with paint as only a four year old can paint. I saved them, and when she was thirty, I showed them to her and said she could take them to her home. She looked at me with a you've-got-to-be-kidding expression and said, "No, thank you." I couldn't believe she didn't want them. In fact, she didn't even remember making them. I decided I would continue to hold on to them for her. One day when I was organizing a closet, I came across the dolls again. This time I took a picture and tossed the dolls. (With some longing, I admit). I downloaded the photo, and the next day, I was going to send it in to have it developed so I could put it in our family photo album. When I looked at the photo I thought, why? Even though it seemed important at one time, I decided I didn't need to keep it forever. It felt good to get rid of clutter and create space. It would have been better if I had taken a photo at the time she made them, with her in the photo. This way I wouldn't have had the clutter all those years, and the photo would have gone in her life book.

> Sometimes we get so caught up in having things, we lose sight of the fact that letting go is the healthy thing to do.

Do not keep things "just in case" you may need them someday. They take up space and create clutter. Ask yourself questions like: How hard would it be to replace this? Would it be cheaper for me to keep it or replace it when I need it? Do I have space to store it? Yes, there is that possibility you could use some of the things you are holding on to, but chances are you will never need them or use them again. I was cleaning out my file cabinet, and I came across a poem. It had been

The Legend of the Phoenix

A phoenix is a mythical bird with a tail of beautiful gold and red plumage (or purple and blue, by some sources). It has a thousand-year life cycle, and near the end, the phoenix builds itself a nest of cinnamon twigs that it then ignites. Both nest and bird burn fiercely and are reduced to ashes, from which a new, young phoenix or phoenix egg arises, reborn to live again.

The story of this beautiful bird that rises out of ashes reminds me that when we organize, there will be chaos and things will actually look worse for a little while (like a big mess you may want to catch fire!). But just like the rising of the phoenix, beauty, organized space and peace of mind will prevail. Your new, organized spaces will rise out of the chaos of your currently disorganized spaces.

in the cabinet for more than twenty-five years, and I had completely forgotten about it. I argued with myself about throwing it away. I finally did and the next week (after garbage day), a friend called to tell me she was giving a talk, and I immediately thought of that poem and how perfect it would be for her talk. I contacted another friend for a copy of the poem and she directed me to a Web site where I might find it. I not only found the poem I wanted, but I now have a great resource to use in the future that does not clutter my space. And it turns out my friend didn't want to use the poem for her talk anyway.

Tip: Don't hold on to a lot of "stuff" you really don't need, and justify it with, "I may need it someday." This thinking is keeping your home at a low wattage.

Brighten Your Thoughts

If you have told yourself that you can't get organized, here is a "light bulb" moment: You can get organized. Change your thoughts to *I want to get organized* and *I can be organized*. You will start to believe it as you see progress—and by following the three simple steps—Searchlight, Spotlight and Green Light—you are on your way.

My daughter participated in a two-day, two-hundred-mile bicycle ride from Seattle, Washington, to Portland, Oregon. The hardest part of her training was the challenging hills; she said they were about killing her. Anytime she saw a hill ahead, she dreaded it. We suggested she change her thinking from how hard the hills were to telling herself she could bike the hills with ease and other positive self-talk. When the ride was over, she said thinking positive had really helped her every time she approached a hill. Every time you start to dread organizing, think to yourself, *I can organize with ease and it will be fun and rewarding* (or, if nothing else, *it will be done and I will be so much happier*). Positive thoughts produce positive feelings. I will be here encouraging you every step of the way.

You have used the Searchlight to find what you want to organize and the Spotlight to determine your goals, and you have a new and positive outlook. Now move on to the chapter with instructions for the room you want to organize first. You don't have to read the chapters in the order they are printed in this book. Let's get started. Green Light ahead!

Entryways

(3)

Our homes can be our sanctuaries, our place of comfort from the stresses of the outside world. Our feelings of welcome and peace begin when we see the exterior of our home and continue as soon as we open the door to the entryway. These areas also create a visitor's first impressions of our homes. Creating an environment that is inviting to both you and your guests is one of the key benefits to organizing. So what better place to start organizing than in your home's welcome center?

Entryways vary from home to home, and many homes have more than one entrance. This chapter deals with all of them, from the back door, "mudroom" entrance to the more formal front door entrance, and the exterior front entryway. Let's start with the exterior entry and work our way in.

Paula's Story

Using her Searchlight, Paula walked to the front of her home and evaluated what kind of impression her home was making for family and guests. She liked the wreath on the door and the welcome mat. She didn't like that the mat was dirty, and there was a broken flower pot with a dead plant in it. Children's toys were all over, and flyers had been left on the porch. She could see that her porch had a cluttered look and did not look inviting. On the wattage scale, she felt it rated a 4.

THE FRONT PORCH

The front porch, or exterior front entrance if you don't have a porch, may be a quick and easy place to start organizing.

Searchlight

Start by getting out your Searchlight and evaluating the area. The Searchlight step is the time for you to look at the space and identify any problems. Decide what you like, what works for you and determine what doesn't work for you or what is keeping you from a wattage that lights you up. In your notebook, make a list of things that you want to change in this space by answering these questions:

1. What do you like about the space?
2. What don't you like about the space? Identify needs by asking these questions:

a. Is the space orderly?

b. Are there things here you could get rid of?

c. Does everything have a home? (Are things contained or scattered around?)

d. Are you keeping only things you use?

e. Do you think this space looks inviting?

3. Now that you have taken a good look at this area, rate your wattage (see page 15). On a scale of 1 to 10 does it light you up on a wattage of 7 or above?

On your porch, you could have a welcome mat, a boot scraper, a container to contain shoes, an umbrella stand, plants, a wreath on the door, or a small table and chairs. Take a picture of this area so you have it for a before-and-after comparison.

Spotlight

After identifying the problem areas, use the Spotlight to consider and focus on what you want your porch to look like. Write down your vision for the porch. Then use that vision to set goals and develop a plan so you will reach your goals. Here are some goals you could set to increase the wattage on your porch:

> A first impression leaves a lasting impression!

1. Keep the porch clean.

2. Keep only beautiful things on the porch.

3. Do not keep toys on the porch.

4. Pick up newspapers and flyers on a daily basis.

If you have large goals that will take a lot of work to achieve, break those goals down into smaller steps that you can work toward. Also set deadlines for when you want to reach your goals.

Green Light

Once you've set your goals, you've got the Green Light to start organizing. This is the step where you take action and make the changes you want! Here are some things you can do to turn up the wattage at your front door:

- Move everything off the porch. This will make it easier to clean, either by sweeping or vacuuming, if you have carpet.
- Place things back on your porch being careful not to get a cluttered look by having too many things in the space you have.
- Make space at your front door for people to stand. This is one place where the expression "less is more" is certainly true. Plants and flowers are beautiful, but if they take over your space, they can also become clutter. Cobwebs are not welcome at the front door (or anywhere else in your home).
- Don't keep empty or broken flowerpots.
- Return gardening tools where they belong; don't keep them on the porch.
- Make a place for outdoor toys to go when not being used. This could be in the garage or at the end of the carport.
- Remove holiday decorations or seasonal items in a timely manner. When decorating for a holiday, plan ahead and mark on your calendar when you will take the decorations down—or better yet, arrange for someone else (like a family member or a professional service) to take them down and put them away.

Wrap Up

Let's chat for a minute about maintaining your newly organized area. With your Searchlight you found the problems, with your Spotlight you created your vision of your desired outcome, and with your Green Light you took action to organize. Share your goals with your family about keeping this area looking clean, organized, and inviting for them and for visitors. Ask them what wattage they think it is. Tell them why you want it to stay this way and enlist their help.

Ask them for suggestions on how they will help to keep it looking nice and inviting. When they are a part of the decision-making process, they will more readily help. After you receive their input, set up some rules. Rotate weekly whose responsibility it will be to keep the area clean and neat. Be sure everyone understands and agrees with the rules. Be sure to praise your family as the weeks go by and the porch stays uncluttered. If you start to see clutter creep in again, take care of it before it becomes a big problem. Go back and discuss the rules everyone agreed to.

A porch kept clean and clear of clutter makes it look well cared for, inviting, and serene (which means unclouded and bright).

FAMILY ENTRANCE

Now that the exterior entrance is organized, it's time to move on to the interior. Let's start by focusing on the entrance you and your family use the most. Not everyone uses their front door. We often access our homes through back or side doors. Some homes have a mudroom attached to the backside entrance, and others have a door that opens directly into the kitchen. Whatever your setup, the entrance that is frequently used can quickly and easily become a magnet for clutter.

This entryway is a high-traffic area that should be organized so it can handle all the activities that take place here. This is where you and your family leave coats, shoes, boots, school papers, keys, and maybe sort the mail. Organizing and having places for everything eliminates (or at least greatly reduces) the problems of clutter and chaos.

Searchlight

Take your Searchlight and start searching for what is working and what isn't working. As always, start your search from the inside out (closets, drawers and storage containers you may have here). Take a picture of this area for a before-and-after comparison.

1. What do you like about this area?
2. What don't you like about this space? Ask yourself these questions:
   a. Is the closet filled with a jumble of coats? Are there coats that don't fit family members anymore?
   b. Are boots and shoes all over the floor and spilling out into the room?
   c. Is there miscellaneous clutter, such as boxes and empty bags, that have been tossed here because you didn't know where to put them?
   d. Is there space to hang up backpacks?
   e. If you sort mail here, is there a landing place for it?
   f. Is there a place for children's school work?
   g. Is there a place for keys?
3. Rate your wattage (see page 15). On a scale of 1 to 10 how does it make you feel?

Spotlight

The Spotlight is where you will set goals for the family entry. Imagine how you want this space to look and write this vision down. You want everything to be accessible and easy to use in order to eliminate clutter and frustration. Set goals you can achieve and maintain. Here are some realistic goals for this area:

1. Make room for coats currently being worn. Come up with a solution to enable younger children to hang up their coats on their own.
2. Contain shoes left in the entryway.

3. Create a landing place for the mail and newspaper.
4. Assign a convenient place for your keys.
5. Set up a place for family members to hang their backpacks, briefcases, and purses.

Remember to break larger goals down into smaller steps and set deadlines for reaching your goals.

Green Light

Now that you know your needs and have set your goals, you can get to work organizing. As you set up your room to make it functional for you, categorize the spaces in it, including the closets, shelves, and open spaces. This entire entryway is premium space because you use it every day (see page 24). Keep only items in this room, or space, that you use regularly. If you do use this area to store other items, be sure you aren't using premium space to do so. Depending on the size of your home's entryway, the following ideas may or may not work for you. You can adjust them to meet your needs and your home's layout. No matter the space, the concepts are the same.

- Along a wall, place a basket, rug or reed mat for shoes. Removing dirty shoes at the door keeps floors cleaner so there is less upkeep.
- A small table can hold a basket for keys, cell phones or other items. If there are young children or visitors in and out of this area, I suggest keeping these items out of their reach. Or if your table has a drawer you can put them in there. For safety's sake, make sure this area is secure so these items aren't stolen or carried away to be played with and lost.
- This is the ideal place to have a cupboard, locker, cubbies, or hooks on the wall to hang coats and backpacks. Assign each family member a hook by placing labels under the hooks. Use a label maker or masking tape to make the labels. These storage items can be purchased at home decorating stores or discount stores.

- Hang a key rack conveniently in the room. Having one place for keys saves time, energy, and frustration as you don't have to hunt to find your keys. If a key hook won't work for you, place a bowl or basket on a flat surface so you can toss your keys and change in it. Again, be aware of safety issues.
- Create a hanging file system that is secured on a wall or use one that sits on a flat surface. This is ideal for children to place their paperwork in as they come home from school. Have a slot for you, too. Anything that needs your attention can be placed in your box and you can review it and take action later.
- Include a garbage can and shredder if you are going to sort mail in this room. Use a basket to hold the mail. How to sort the mail will be discussed in depth in Chapter 11.
- If this room has closet space, it may be the ideal room to store out-of-season coats, gloves, and scarves. Store small items in a basket or plastic container and keep these containers on the closet shelf. Sports equipment and clothing could be placed in labeled bins and stored in the closet as well.
- An over-the-door organizer with pockets (typically used for shoes) can be used for keys, sunglasses, gloves, hats, scarves, a camera and other electronic equipment, leashes for dogs, and other miscellaneous items. The pockets can be labeled with family members' names. Reserve the lower rows for younger children. The organizer keeps things contained and convenient to grab and go when leaving the house.

FRONT OR FORMAL ENTRYWAY

This is the entryway your visitors use. It is where they form their first impression of your home. Creating a warm welcome that is inviting to both you and your guests is important when stepping into this space.

Searchlight

Take a look around with the Searchlight and ask yourself what is it you like and what you don't like. Be honest in your evaluation, but don't beat yourself up. As you use your Searchlight, make a list in your notebook of things that you need to change in this area. Formal entryways often have a closet. If you have a closet in your entryway, this is the place to start. What do you see when you open the closet door? Are there so many coats on the rod that it's difficult to remove a coat to wear? Are there scarves, gloves, and coats tossed on the floor? Take a picture of this area for a before-and-after comparison.

1. What do you like most about the space?
2. What don't you like about the space? Identify needs by asking yourself these questions:
   a. Is the space orderly?
   b. Are there things here you could get rid of?
   c. Does everything have a home? (Are items contained or scattered around?)
   d. Are you keeping only the items you use?
   e. Are items that belong somewhere else scattered around?
   f. Do all of the coats, shoes, gloves, and mittens in the closet fit someone in the house?
3. How did the closet get in this shape?
4. Rate your wattage (see page 15). On a scale of 1 to 10, how do you feel when you're in this area?

Spotlight

You have found things you don't like, and you want to change them and make your entryway better. With the Spotlight, set goals that will make this area warm and welcoming for family and guests. Here are some possible goals for this area:

1. Make room for coats currently being worn. Donate coats you no longer use. In the future, get rid of an old coat when you buy a new one.
2. Purchase a container to hold the scarves, gloves, and hats.
3. Contain shoes left in the entryway.
4. Keep the table clutter-free.
5. Teach family members to use the "mudroom" entry so everything is in one area. Less traffic will also make the area easier to maintain.

Green Light

This is the fun part when you see your goals realized. You have written down your goals for this space and now you get to work on them. Sit down with your family and explain the goals for the formal entryway in your home. Get their ideas on how to keep it organized. Then get their commitment to help. Stick to your organizing goals.

Some things to consider having in the front entry are:

- A mirror. It will visually make the area appear larger, and the bonus is you can check your appearance before answering the door.
- A small table. Don't clutter it with keys, cell phones, or other items. Keep these things near your most-used entrance. If they have to be kept here, contain them in an attractive container.
- Keep furniture to a minimum to create the look of spaciousness.
- A shoe rack or a basket to hold shoes.
- An umbrella stand.

Here are some more ideas that can help you organize the entryway:

1. In the closet, only keep the family's dress coats, leaving enough room for guests' coats.
2. Store seasonal hats, gloves, and scarves in a basket and place it on the top shelf. Or store these in the family's entry room.

3. Keep a container near the front door or in the closet for shoes that are removed when coming in the house.
4. Provide a basket elsewhere in the home for the newspaper.
5. On the small table, place a plant or family photos and inform everyone these are the only things that are to be placed on top of the table. It is not a dumping ground or catchall for the mail, books, or other items. Limit the number of framed photos on this table to three as you don't want the table to look cluttered.

Wrap Up

Inside, the front entryway is now clutter-free and visually appealing. In the family entrance, there are places for keys, everyday coats, books, shoes, newspapers and other miscellaneous items, or you have designated other places for these items. The entryways are no longer clutter magnets or dumping areas as there is a place for everything, and everything will be in its place.

Your entryways will always be welcoming as you continue to:

- Keep the porch clean and free of debris.
- Keep only beautiful things on the porch.
- Pick up newspapers and flyers on a daily basis.
- Use the places designated for coats, keys, books, shoes, newspapers, and other miscellaneous items.
- Keep flat surfaces free of clutter.

Your home has a welcoming and warm feeling when stepping into your entry. What is your wattage rating now? Take another photo. Look back at the before photo and feel good about your progress. Way to go. I am proud of you. I knew you could do it!

(4) The Living Room

The living room is also known as the front room because it is often the first room people walk into when they enter your home. It is a place where people can sit, talk, and relax. It is usually a room used for entertaining guests, reading, and other activities. This makes it an important room as it gives people an impression of what kind of person you are, so you want it to reflect positively on you and your family. This chapter doesn't cover organizing an entertainment center. If you have an entertainment center in you living room, see Chapter 10, Family Room, for advice on organizing areas dealing with a television, DVDs, and CDs.

The History of the Living Room

The living room has replaced the old-fashioned parlor. In the nineteenth century, the parlor was the room in the house where the recently deceased were laid out before their funeral. In the twentieth century the term "living room" was made popular by architects and builders to change from the parlor's mourning associations. (Aren't we glad?)

SEARCHLIGHT

Take the Searchlight and look for things that are working and things that aren't working. Write each of these down in your notebook. What is keeping you from a wattage that lights you up when you walk in your living room? Now is a good time to take a picture while you are assessing your room. Ask yourself:

1. What do you like about this room?
2. What don't you like about this room? Identify needs by asking yourself the following questions:
   a. What is the function or purpose of this room? Is this a room with a piano? Are other musical instruments played here? Do children play with toys here?
   b. Are you embarrassed when visitors come to your home? Do you always apologize because of the clutter, and do visitors have to stand while you remove it from the chairs and couch so they will have a place to sit?
   c. Do you display any collections here, perhaps fragile figurines?

How does the display look? Can you see everything and enjoy it, or does it look cluttered and over-flowing?

d. Are there too many pieces of furniture in the room for its size?

e. Is the space orderly? Do the items in this room each have a "home"?

f. Are there things you can get rid of?

g. Are the children's toys organized/contained?

h. Do the flat surfaces (tabletops, piano, mantel, fireplace hearth) have clutter on them? (This could be mail, sheet music, keys, bags, purses, newspaper and magazines, musical instruments, etc.) Is this a catchall room for things that belong in other rooms such as dishes, books, coats, backpacks, or clothing?

i. Does each item you have in this room light you up to a 7 or above?

j. How did your living room get in this shape?

3. Now that you have taken a good look at this room, rate your wattage (see page 15). When you are in this room, are you lit up at a 7 or above?

Once you have answered these questions and written your answers in your notebook, move on to using the Spotlight to set goals.

Tip: *When decorating for the holidays, remove objects that are out year-round. For short-term storage, place them in the holiday boxes as you take out the holiday decorations. Then, when you take down the holiday decorations, you can place the year-round objects back out on display.*

SPOTLIGHT

You did a really great job analyzing your living room and identifying problem areas. Now with the Spotlight, focus on setting goals to make this room what you want it to be. You wrote down the problem areas; now write down your

Paula's Story

When Paula used her Searchlight in her living room, she was surprised at what she saw. She usually avoided this room. There were newspapers scattered on the couch and floor. The fabric was stained from the newspapers and spilled drinks. Magazines were piled on tables and catalogs were in several places. She wondered why she even subscribed to so many magazines. She never had time to read them. Children's toys were all over the floor, chairs, and fireplace hearth. Her children's piano and clarinet sheet music overflowed from the piano bench and was left lying on the floor and on top of the piano. She took an objective look at the room and realized she had too much furniture for the space. It made the room look cluttered, even though they were nice pieces of furniture. Books were not put back in the bookcase, and their paper covers were ripped and shoddy looking.

Her doll collection took up a lot of space in the room, but she couldn't see most of it because the dolls were crammed close together and behind each other in curio cabinets. She didn't enjoy the way they looked, and they made the room look cluttered.

Dirty dishes were on the tables and floor. How many times, she wondered, had she told her family that if they were going to eat in the living room, they would have to take the dishes back to the kitchen.

The holidays were coming. She wanted to display her beautiful decorations, but the decorations only added to the cluttered look. There was nowhere to put them.

On the wattage scale, she felt the room rated a 3. There were things she liked in the room, and she liked what the room was used for, but she was ready to make changes.

goals. As you accomplish each one, you can check it off. Here are some examples of goals you could set for this room:

1. Guests will feel welcome, and you won't be embarrassed to have visitors.
2. Remove extra furniture. Quality is more important than quantity. Arrange furniture in an orderly way, giving the room a feeling of space and comfort. Keep folding chairs handy for extra seating or purchase an ottoman that can serve as seating, as well as a table and a storage container.
3. Look at each item in the room and get rid of or replace everything that doesn't have a wattage of 7 or above. You can replace items over a period of time.
4. Keep all flat surfaces clutter-free. To do this: use containers; give everything a home within the room; and place items that don't belong in the room in a proper home in another room.
5. Contain children's toys in a basket.
6. Place convenient containers for magazines, newspapers, and music in the room.
7. Organize books on the bookshelf; make room for the books that need to be kept in this room. Remove paper dustcovers from the books.
8. Remove part of the collections in the room and store the items in semi-storage (see page 24). Purchase proper storage containers if needed. Know where you will store these items before you pack them up.
9. Hang pictures to brighten and beautify the room.
10. Educate family members on what can and cannot be left in the living room. Show them the new places for all of the objects that have been removed from the room. Your family probably won't say, "Oh goodie, we'll never leave our socks, shoes, and other stuff here again." It will take some training and maybe consequences to see lasting results.

Be sure to write down a target date to complete these goals.

GREEN LIGHT

Your goals are set; you now have the Green Light to take action. Have a good time and take it as slow as you need to. To stay focused wear comfortable clothes, have your tool kit (see page 22), and use the four containers method (see page 35). Get a drink and a snack. You are ready to turn up the wattage in your living room.

Schedule a time to start working. Set your timer for a specific amount of time. If you are the type of person who has to get it all done right now, set your timer for one hour. If twenty minutes is all you can do, set your timer for twenty minutes, and so on. Getting started and making a dent is better than never starting. When the timer dings, if you are in a comfortable rhythm and have time to continue working, set your timer again and keep going. When you need to take a break, set your timer for five minutes so you'll remember to come back.

As always, start working from the inside out. Remember, things will look worse before they look better.

Places to start:

1. curio cabinets
2. bookshelves
3. piano bench
4. storage containers, such as toy boxes, ottomans and baskets
5. built-in storage shelves or armoires
6. flat surfaces such as:
    a. tabletops (e.g., coffee tables and end tables)
    b. fireplace mantel and hearth
    c. top of the piano
7. furniture
8. pillows and blankets

Use your four containers to quickly manage the things you aren't going to keep in this room.

Managing Your Magazines

If you subscribe to magazines you don't read, cancel your subscriptions. Many articles from magazines can be found online. If there are articles from magazines you have that you want to save, create a resource book. Tear out the article, slip it into a plastic sleeve and place it in a three-ring binder. Separate each section by using page dividers. These can be separated alphabetically or by subject. Keep current magazines contained in a magazine rack or basket. Every three months, throw the old ones away, and do the same with catalogs. If the entire magazine is a resource (like business or craft magazines) keep them in a magazine holder you can place in a book case. Be sure to label the holders with magazine names and year.

Tip: All things need a home, and they need to live in their home when not in use. If you follow this principle, you'll always know where things are and you'll never waste time looking for things. Is your home so organized that you could get up in the middle of the night, and find what you need in the dark?

Curio Cabinet: Dust the items in the curio cabinet. If it looks cramped and cluttered, pack up some of the items and place them in semi-storage. (Wrap them in bubble wrap or in packing paper to keep them from getting broken.) Rotate the items in and out about every six months to a year. If they no longer light you up to a 7 or above, remove them from the room. Consider selling them or giving them to family members.

Bookshelves: Sort through the books on the bookshelves. If there are books no one reads or your family has outgrown, donate or sell them. Now organize the rest. It is okay to throw away the paper dust jackets; they get tattered and make the shelves look messy.

Piano Bench: If there is too much sheet music to fit, keep only the pieces currently being used here. The rest can be put in magazine holders and placed on the bookcase, stacked upright between bookends, placed in a basket or open container, or stored in a container on a closet shelf. If they are never used any more, donate them to a piano teacher, school, or charity.

Storage Containers: Look at the containers in the room and if they don't fit the atmosphere you want, change the containers. An ottoman can be used for storing magazines or toys, and you can also use it for a foot rest or extra seating. Dump out the toy boxes or baskets and evaluate each toy before putting it back into the container. This is a good time to donate toys the children no longer play with or have outgrown. In this room, only keep the amount of toys that can fit in a designated container. The baskets holding magazines and catalogs need to be cleaned out at least every three months. Recycle the old ones as you get new ones.

Built-In Storage Shelves or Armoires: Take everything off the shelves one shelf at a time. Dust the shelves and evaluate everything you place back in this space. If you no longer enjoy the item, donate it, or if you want to keep it, rotate the items in and out of the shelves about every six months.

Tabletops: Take everything off the tabletops and dust them. These are such easy places to put papers, dishes, glasses, and other things! Place a basket near the tables to put the newspaper in and another basket for magazines. Mail is no longer allowed in this room; it will go directly to the office or another room where you sort mail. Children's school work will be contained in the designated area in the family's entryway. They can bring out homework to work on, but it goes back to their backpacks as soon as it is finished. Limit what you will place

You Never Know What You'll Find

I took my own advice, and in my living room, I put to the test the working-from-the-inside-out principle. I was laughing when I opened my piano bench and soon my confident I-know-only-sheet-music-is-here attitude vanished. Much to my surprise, I found catalogs, a book, a scarf, a half-eaten candy bar, and gloves. The candy went into the trash, and everything else went in the belongs-elsewhere basket. With those distractions immediately out of the way, I was able to focus on organizing the bench's contents.

on the tabletops to lamps and up to three to five decorative items, depending on the size of the table.

Mantel and Hearth: Take everything off the fireplace mantel and hearth and dust them. Only put back those things that light you up. Donate, sell, store, or give away objects you don't want to keep out on display.

Top of the Piano: Remove everything from the top of the piano and dust it. Put back the things you love, being careful not to get it cluttered. If you like to display pictures here, only put back half of the number you had on display; limit them to your favorites. Put the other pictures in an album.

Furniture: Remove any broken furniture by placing it near the doorway of the room to either be taken to a shop to be repaired or to be donated. Remove excess furniture that isn't used. If you decide to donate the furniture, some charities will arrange to pick up the donations at your home, making it easier for you. If you sell the furniture, stipulate that the purchaser must pick up the item and transport it from your home.

Don't Overwhelm Small Spaces

If your living room is the "company room" and is very small, less furniture will make it appear larger. Keep folding chairs in the storage room for extra seating. Hanging mirrors on the walls can make the room look longer or wider. Keep items like photos, magazines, or figurines placed on the tables to a minimum. End tables with shelves underneath can be a place to store things like books and magazines if you also use this for a reading room.

Pillows and Blankets: Keep throw pillows on the chairs or couches. Pillows can create a cluttered look if they are strewn around the room on the floor. If someone in your home insists on throwing them on the floor, the rule could be that they put them back on the couch when they leave the room. You could have pillows designated to stay on the couch and place others in a basket when not in use. Limit the number of pillows you have on your furniture so people have enough room to sit. Have a designated home for blankets used in this room. Use a container for the blankets, such as a basket placed at the end of the couch, behind the couch, or on one end of the hearth away from the fireplace opening. Ask family members to fold blankets and put them away when they are done using them.

Hang some favorite pictures to make the room feel welcoming to both family and friends.

Check the goals you wrote down and take a few moments to enjoy the feeling of how much you accomplished. You did a great job! It is good to give yourself a pat on the back! Share your accomplishment with someone else.

Tip: Make your room smell fresh and clean by dusting the furniture with a scented polish that you like, or keep a candle on a candle warmer.

WRAP UP

The living room is usually the first room people see when they enter your home. Make it a room that is inviting, comfortable, and welcoming. Now that it is organized, everything has a designated home and excess items have been removed, cleaning this area becomes less of a chore. It truly is a place to welcome your guests.

So how do you keep the room just as you want it? Every night before going to bed take three to five minutes to put things away and tidy up. You can do it yourself every night or rotate this responsibility among family members (which is what I suggest doing). When family members share the responsibility of maintaining the organization, they will soon start putting back what they use, and you'll need less time to straighten up the area. It is easier for everyone when everything has a designated place to live.

Your living room will stay organized because:

- The room is "straightened up" every night before going to bed.
- The curio cabinet is not overloaded with stuff.
- Flat surfaces are kept free of clutter.
- Only things that light you up are in this room.
- Children's toys, newspapers, blankets, and magazines are contained in baskets.

Doesn't it feel good to have a 10-watt room? You did it. I knew you could. Good job!

The Kitchen

(5)

Do you like walking into your kitchen and preparing meals or snacks for yourself and your family? Is it the place your family gathers after a busy day to unwind and chat about the day's events? Do you find when friends come over to visit, you sit around the kitchen table? The kitchen has been called "the heart of the home." Our hearts are where our feelings of love come from. The kitchen is often the nerve center for activities in the home.

Does your kitchen have a welcoming feeling, or is it so cramped and crowded that it has become a place you dread spending time? If that's the case, let's turn your "lights on" by making it a room you look forward to preparing and cooking food in with family and friends.

SEARCHLIGHT

The Searchlight step is when you take a good look at the kitchen to see what you like and what you don't like. What are the problems that keep this room from working for you and making it a place you like to be? As you use your Searchlight, look thoughtfully at what is working and what isn't working for you. Write a list of things you want to change in your notebook. Take a picture of the full kitchen and inside of each cupboard and drawer. Write down responses to the following questions in your notebook:

1. What do you like about this room?
2. What don't you like about this room? Here are some questions to help you identify your needs:
   a. Are the counters free from clutter (i.e., papers, books, dishes, etc.)?
   b. Does this room look inviting? Do you feel comfortable here?
   c. Are the cupboards crowded and in disarray?
   d. Is there space in the drawers for the utensils or is everything jumbled together?
   e. Is there a designated place for everything?
   f. Are the "junk" drawers junky, or are things easy to find? Is it more of a lost-and-found drawer?
   g. Is the refrigerator and freezer organized so you can find specific items and use them before they spoil?
   h. Is the floor free of debris and the garbage emptied?
   i. Are you keeping only things you use or are you keeping extra things "just in case" you need them someday? Are there things you never use and don't like, yet you keep them?
   j. Are the dishes in a convenient location, relative to the dishwasher, for loading and unloading?
   k. Are container lids "contained" or are they exploding out of the cupboard or drawer?

Paula's Story

Paula used her Searchlight and began looking carefully through the inside of her kitchen cupboards and on the countertops. At first, she loved what she saw; the counters were clear except for the juicer, the bread maker, the ice cream maker, and a large slow cooker—all of which she rarely used. She knew they took up a lot of valuable space, but she had learned to live with them and didn't know what else to do with the appliances. She began looking through the kitchen cupboards and saw that each cupboard she opened was piled with bowls her family didn't use, and some dishes were cracked. There were too many mugs, pans were topsy-turvy, and the lids were stacked unevenly, often falling out. The plastic and glass containers had lids that she found scattered in different cupboards. She realized she didn't know if all the bowls even had matching lids or if there were more lids than bowls. In the refrigerator, things were hard to find, and there was a lot of spoiled food that had been shoved toward the back. Many items like the milk, jam, and ketchup, were never put away in the same place. After using her Searchlight, she decided her kitchen was only 4.5 on the wattage scale.

l. Do infrequently used appliances take up valuable counter space?

m. Are the canned goods and other food products near the cooking area?

n. Are pans stored in a convenient place for cooking?

3. Now that you have taken a good look at the space in this room (both

inside and out), rate your wattage for this room (see page 15). If you rated the wattage in this room as a 7 or above, the room lights you up, and you feel happy, peaceful, and calm when you're in the room. If you rated it as a 4 or below, you feel tense, out of sorts, uncomfortable, and agitated when you're in the room.

SPOTLIGHT

You have written down what isn't working for you, and you have identified the specific problem areas, such as cluttered counters, lack of space in the cupboards, a messy junk drawer that isn't usable, container lids scattered all over so you can't find the right one when you want it, and spoiled food in the refrigerator. Now you are ready to set goals and develop a plan to reach your goals. Here are some examples of goals you can set for the kitchen that will increase the wattage in the room:

1. Keep the counters free of unnecessary appliances and paper clutter.
2. Make more room in the cupboards for the items you use most often.
3. Organize the pantry by labeling the shelves if necessary and assigning designated areas for everything.
4. Organize the junk drawer to make it a resource drawer by adding containers or dividers.
5. Get rid of duplicate utensils. Only keep what you use. Add drawer dividers.
6. Remove infrequently used appliances to semi-storage areas.
7. Designate a convenient place for trash.
8. Organize the refrigerator to have like items together.
9. Keep dishes you use every day in the most convenient place.
10. Use containers to hold lids for bowls that have them.
11. Get rid of all broken utensils and chipped, broken, or cracked dishes.
12. Organize spices and check expiration.

13. Organize under the sink.
14. Buy expandable shelves to increase space in cupboards. (These can be purchased at local home stores, discount stores, or perhaps hardware stores.)

Write down the target date when you want to have these goals completed. Break the goals down into sections—cupboards, counters, refrigerator—doing one at a time over the course of a couple of days, or working two hours (or more) a day, until the kitchen is just how you want it to be.

Great job! That was quite a project to thoroughly look through your kitchen and set your goals for change! You are on your way to making your kitchen look and feel like a 10-watt room!

GREEN LIGHT

Now you are going to use your goals and take action. (Can you feel the excitement mounting?) You will have a great time transforming and improving your counters', and cupboards', appearance and functionality. A word of caution: Things will look worse before they look better. We are always being told, be neat, be clean, de-clutter, don't make a mess. This is one time when you can make a big mess and it is OK. Take heart; this is the Lights On Organizing System to a better, more organized kitchen.

Use the Green Light by wearing comfortable clothes and rounding up your tool kit (see page 22) and four containers (see page 35). Because you're in the kitchen, your drink and snacks are handy.

> "Best way to get rid of kitchen odors: Eat out."
>
> —PHYLLIS DILLER

Schedule a time when there will be the fewest interruptions for you to begin. Set your timer, and if your family is home, let them know you are working in the kitchen for a minimum of thirty minutes to one hour and to leave you alone! Let them know you won't be answering the phone; you can call the person back later. After you have worked for your set time, keep going if you can, and reset your timer. You will feel energized with every cupboard you clear out and see organized. When you take a break, set your timer for five minutes to remind you to come back.

This is such a great room to work from the inside out. Open up your cupboards and start inside them first, and then move to the outside spaces. It doesn't matter which cupboard you choose first, but here are my suggestions on where to start:

1. Upper cupboards
   a. glasses
   b. dishes/bowls
   c. over the stove
   d. over the refrigerator
2. Utensil drawers
3. Lower cupboards
   a. pots and pans
   b. under the sink
   c. bulky appliances; muffin tins, cookie sheets
   d. baking supplies; cupboard with food
4. Pantry
5. Junk drawer
6. Countertops
7. Refrigerator and freezer

Be absolutely honest with yourself as you look at each item. In order to keep it, you have to like it enough that it lights you up at a 7 or above on the wattage scale (see page 15).

Upper Cupboards

Glasses and Cups Cupboard: Take everything out. Wipe out the cupboard. Put the glasses in the cupboard next to or near the sink if that is where you usually use them. If you get your water from the refrigerator along with other beverages, put your glasses in the cupboard where they are most convenient to be used and to be loaded and unloaded from the dishwasher. If you don't have a cupboard for glasses only, put them on the shelf above or below the dishes. Be sure you are only keeping the ones you like and that aren't chipped or broken. You are at risk of injury by using chipped or cracked glasses (even if it was your favorite one from your aunt). Throw away those old, ugly, plastic mugs and glasses you don't like and don't enjoy using but you do use them because they are in the cupboard. (These include the souvenir and promotional cups you get from businesses and restaurants.) They aren't going to break, so they aren't going to go away; they can outlast you so go ahead, be brave and recycle them. (No one else will want them either, so don't bother donating them.)

This is premium space, so only keep the amount of glasses that your family uses on a daily basis. Other glasses can go to other shelves considered secondary space. (See page 24 to review premium and secondary spaces.)

Tip: *Do you have the "never-any-clean-glasses-in-the-house" syndrome? Buy different colored glasses for each family member, or put a different colored elastic band around each glass assigning a different color for each user. Ask family members to reuse their glass as often as possible throughout the day. The different colored glasses should help them do this.*

Dishes and Bowls: Take everything out and wipe out the cupboard. Throw away any plates and bowls that are chipped or broken and get rid of the ones that rate 6 and below on the wattage scale.

Stack the dinner plates in one pile, the salad plates in another, and the bowls in another. This is where additional shelves are nice because they eliminate the pain and bother of removing one size of plates to get to another. (See *Extra Shelves in Cupboards* on page 77 for more information.)

Storage Options for Leftovers

If you store your leftovers in plastic containers that had other products in them, such as margarine, cottage cheese, or yogurt, here are some guidelines. Don't use them. Recycle the plastic some other way than by storing food in them because:

1. You can't see in them, so often the food spoils before it is used.

2. They don't stack as well as containers uniform in size, thus taking up more space in the refrigerator.

3. Some plastics, when heated in the microwave, warp or melt possibly causing harmful chemicals to leach into the food. Older plastics tend to leach increasing amounts of toxins as they age. On the bottom of plastic containers is a number. When you need to use plastic, these are the safer choices to use with food: 1, 2, 4, and 5. Avoid numbers 3, 6, and 7.

4. These "freebie" types of containers have babies, multiplying and dividing faster than rabbits. If you must use them, make a rule that you will not keep more than five to ten (depending on the size of your family) of them in your cupboards. The other ones go to the recycle bin after using the product in them. They can also be used to store nonfood items.

Honestly, do these yellow, white, (ugly) containers light you up on a scale of 7 or above? That is always your criteria when deciding if something is to be kept in your home. I know these containers are free, but it isn't about the cost, it is about how you feel. A much safer and more attractive choices for leftover containers are glass, pottery, crockery, and stainless steel.

Keep dishes that you use most often in the easiest-to-reach places where they are most convenient to use and to put back in the cupboard after they are washed. Move the dishes you don't use daily to secondary spaces. This could be to a higher cupboard. Serving pieces can also go on higher shelves if they aren't used on a daily basis.

Take out all bowls that have lids. (This should include serving bowls with lids and plastic containers you use for leftovers.) Match lids to the bowls. If there are bowls without lids or lids without bowls, put these orphans in a plastic bag. Label the bag "missing bowls/lids." Keep the bag for one week (the orphans might be in a bedroom or some other place in the house). If matches haven't been found in a week, recycle the bowls and lids.

> **Tip:** *Plan two weeks to thirty days of menus at one time. From these menus, you can make your shopping list, and you will have a nice variety of dinners planned so meal time doesn't get boring. It will save you time and the frustration of wondering "what is for dinner tonight." It takes the dread out of preparing dinner. There are a lot of preplanned menus available on the Internet that you can use for inspiration.*

Over the Stove: Take everything out of this cupboard and wipe it out. This way you can see what you have. This is such a tricky cupboard because, if you're not tall (which I am not), it is hard to get in and out of this cupboard easily. Do not store things here that would be a magnet for children to get into. If they think there are treats there, they will do their best to reach them and could be burned or sustain other injuries. Store things you might not use very often, such as seasonal dishes, plastic and paper products, wine glasses, pie tins, round cake pans, or vases. You decide what you want to keep in this semi-storage area.

Over the Refrigerator: Take everything out and wash the shelves. Possible uses for this cupboard include wine storage, cookie sheets, muffin tins, cookie cutters, cake decorating supplies, and other items you don't use often. I recommend keeping a small, sturdy step stool handy to reach things in this cupboard and other cupboards that are too high to get into easily.

Utensil Drawers

Use a utensil holder for your flatware. The holders with a compartment in the back have room for the corn picks, vegetable peeler, measuring spoons, or ice cream scoops. If the holder slides around, use wide, double-stick tape or a nonslip mat under it to hold it in place.

Large utensils can be kept in a nice container, like a crock, on the counter. If you keep them in a drawer, use drawer dividers to separate the spoons from the spatulas, the hand grater and cheese slicer, and other types of utensils. Dividers will keep everything from sliding around and getting lost and jumbled.

If you don't have enough drawers or your space is limited, a utensil rack can be hung on the wall that has hooks attached to it. Using a pegboard is also an option. It can be mounted on the wall and hooks installed to free up cupboard

Extra Shelves in Cupboards

To create more cupboard space, you can easily install additional shelves by buying removable stainless steel or wire shelves (that are covered in white plastic). These are available at discount stores, kitchen stores, and variety stores. Depending on your needs and cupboard size and shape, there are many types of shelves to increase cupboard space. There are corner shelves, expanding shelves, wide shelves, and narrow shelves. Step shelves look like small stairs. This style of shelf works well to accommodate spices, or canned goods. These will double your cupboard space and make the items placed in the back easier to find.

space for cups, soup bowls, and cooking utensils. Pegboard can easily be painted to match your kitchen décor or the kitchen walls. The one thing I caution about using a pegboard is if you hang too many things on it, the kitchen will look cluttered. So if you use a pegboard, limit the amount of items you hang on it.

Keep sharp knives in plastic sleeves for safety and to avoid nicking the blade, or place them in a wooden butcher block made for knives.

If you have space, a drawer could hold baking utensils such as measuring spoons and cups. You also can place these utensils in a plastic container that easily slides in and out of a cupboard. This is effective for someone in a wheelchair or who has limited range of motion.

You have now gone through all of the upper cupboards and drawers in your kitchen. You have taken everything out of every cupboard, cleaned the shelves, and rearranged some things to make them more functional for you. You have

Solutions for Small Kitchens

If you live in a small apartment or house and your kitchen is the size of a postage stamp, you can make room for dishes, cups, and glasses by installing different types of shelves on your walls. One shelf should have slots to hold plates. You could store large serving bowls on top of the shelf.

The other shelf should have a flat top and sturdy hooks beneath it. You can place drinking glasses on top and hang mugs on the hooks underneath. You also can install appliances like microwaves, can openers, radios, and televisions beneath cupboards to free up counter space.

used containers to contain spices, baking supplies, and lids. Doesn't it just make you want to open your cupboards and see how nice they look? What a great feeling!

Lower Cupboards

Pots and Pans: Pots and pans are more convenient to use when stored on roll-out shelves or deep slide-out drawers. You can install these shelves yourself or have a professional install them for you. Big-box hardware stores carry them. They are nice because they can slide out so the pans are easier to see and reach. These shelves are particularly helpful for people in wheelchairs. You can use the full space in the cupboard because items in the back of the cupboard are easy to reach when you pull out the shelf.

Donate pans you don't use. Throw away pans with warped bottoms or that have been burned beyond repair. Don't keep any pan you can't or don't use. Remember, look at them and assign them a wattage. They have to be a 7 or above to keep. Nest pans together by size. Keep the ones you use most often towards the front of the shelf.

Lids are often a problem. Here are a few options of what to do to contain them: Turn them upside down on the pans; stack them in a wire, plastic, or rattan basket; or stack them on a metal lid rack that hangs on a door or sits inside a cupboard. Some stoves have a drawer under them; this is a good place for lids.

Under the Sink: Move hazardous items to "higher ground," away from children, or child-proof the cupboard by using child-proof locks. Do not put any paper products or other items here that may get ruined from moisture. To increase the space of this cupboard, place a shelf on one side. There are special under-the-sink shelf systems that fit around pipes and add more storage space. A slide-out under-sink organizer can also increase space and accessibility.

In the front, place items together that you regularly use—dish soap, scouring pads, garbage bags, and rubber gloves. Keep items used less frequently (e.g., silver polish, extra soap, floor cleaner, or window cleaner) in a container, such as a caddy or basket, toward the back of the cupboard.

If you opt for the shelf on one side, you can put your trash can on the other side. A slide-out trashcan holder is another option. If you have space in the kitchen, use a trash can with a lid that opens by stepping on a pedal or has a pop-up lid. Use one that is easy to get into so it will be used, and you'll avoid the frustration of having to touch the lid every time to open it.

Bulky Appliances: Keep only the appliances you use at least every six months. If you have an appliance you would like to use but you never do, start scheduling times to use it. If you never follow through with using it, donate it so someone else can enjoy it. You will never miss the appliance. You will enjoy the freedom of space and the freedom from feeling guilty that you don't use it but think you should. If you are having a hard time deciding if you should keep an item, give it a number on the wattage scale to help you decide. Only keep those that are a 7 or above.

Find a place other than on your counter for your bulky appliances that you do use at least twice a month. If you use a large appliance every day, then it makes more sense to keep it on your counter. Things like a bread maker, toaster oven, juicer, or large mixer can be moved to the pantry, a shelf in the garage, or in a lower cupboard if there is room. An armoire in a nearby room may also make a great storage place. A baker's rack can work as well.

Muffin tins and cookie sheets can be stored above the refrigerator if you don't use them weekly or in a cupboard with slots made for this purpose. Some stoves have a drawer under the oven, and they could be stored here.

Tip: Here's a method to get cookie sheets and muffin tins to stand up in a cupboard. Measure your cupboard from the top to the bottom. Then purchase two expandable curtain rods that fit your cupboard's measurements. Place one rod in the front of the cupboard about 3" (8cm) from the front edge and the other rod 8" (20cm) to 12" (30cm) directly behind the first rod in a straight line.

When you store your cookie sheets, cutting boards, trays, or muffin tins, they will stand up between the wall and these rods.

Baking Supplies and Other Food: Take all of your baking supplies and other food out of the cupboards and wipe out the shelves. Before putting the items back in the cupboard, check expiration dates on all items and throw away the expired ones. Wash off the outside of any containers that have gotten grungy. If you have baking supplies like nuts, chocolate chips, or other items that come in bags, put them in containers as they will stack better and take up less space. To prevent nuts from turning rancid (because of their natural oils), store them in an airtight container in the refrigerator or in the freezer where they will last for up to a year. If stored in the refrigerator, they will last half as long as in the freezer because they may be exposed to moisture.

If you use a lazy Susan for your spices or condiments and it is stained or a color you don't like anymore, now is the time to get a new one. You will be amazed at what a difference it makes to see a new one when you open your cupboard.

Tip: *Organizing spices alphabetically makes locating them fast and easy. Smell all of your spices before you put them back in the cupboard. If you can't smell them or they aren't as strong as they used to be, they've lost flavor and you need to replace them.*

Depending on the size and location of your pantry, work hand-in-hand organizing your canned food, boxes of prepared food, and other food items that are in your cupboards along with your pantry. In the pantry, you can keep more food items, and if it is a walk-in pantry, bulky appliances can be kept in it. Keep your most-often-used foods in your cupboards and use your pantry to store more of the same items and food that comes in larger sizes.

Pantry

Take everything out shelf by shelf and put likes together on the table or counter. Wash the shelves and, as you put items back, check the expiration dates on all canned goods and packages or anything else that has expiration dates. Contain items like pasta, mixes, seasonings pouches, and chips in baskets or plastic containers and label these containers. Have a place for everything and label those places on the shelf. When you are out of an item, there is still a space for it when you purchase more. This works for other items as well.

Tip: If you buy food items in bulk, separate the packages into smaller sizes and only keep a month's supply in the pantry or cupboard. The rest can be stored elsewhere in containers with tight-fitting lids to keep out humidity and bugs if these are a problem where you live. They could be stored in an armoire or on a closet shelf. If heat and humidity isn't a concern, they could be stored on a shelf in the garage.

Keep all like items together: Pasta (contain in a container) and boxed items such as cake mixes and pancake mixes, crackers, cereals all go together. Canned goods can be placed together by type in rows on another shelf. Vegetables can be together in one area, soup in another, and canned fruit in another. Put the newer cans or boxes in back and rotate the older items to the front.

Keep the things you use most often in the easiest to reach and to see places—in the premium space (see to page 24). Place large items like olive oil, vinegar, and bottled sauces on a turntable or lazy Susan. They will be easier for you to reach and to see what you have. If these are extra items, store them in secondary spaces, easy to get to but not some place you need to access daily.

Place miscellaneous products together. Things like wax paper, foil, and plastic wraps. Plastic storage bags of all sizes can be placed in containers to keep them all together. This also makes it easier to put them back. For some reason, it is easier to get things out than it is to put them back, so you want to make it as convenient as possible to return things to the designated area. If you have room in a kitchen drawer or cupboard, paper products can be placed there and the extras kept in the pantry.

Tip: Label the shelves in the pantry so everyone will know where the designated place is for each item. They can put things on the shelves after a trip to the store because they know where they belong. It saves time and space, and the pantry stays organized.

Spices could be stored in the pantry on your new turntable or lazy Susan, or on a wall-mounted rack on the inside of the pantry door. Canisters of flour, sugar, and other dry goods can also be kept in the pantry. What you keep in your pantry depends on the size of your kitchen and pantry. If you kitchen is small and your pantry is just a small closet and is a part of your cupboards, then what you put here will be what you frequently use. If you have a walk-in pantry, this will be the place you will store more paper products, food items, and extra things that you use in the kitchen.

Tip: When you are checking the expiration dates on your cans of food and boxed items, or you if are just looking to see what you have, and you find an item you have had for a long time but it hasn't expired, make a menu to use that specific food that week. If you don't plan on using it, donate it to your local food bank.

Junk Drawer

When you're through with this drawer, you'll be calling it a resource drawer. Take everything out and wipe it clean. Junk drawers, lost-and-hopefully-found drawers (a.k.a. resource drawers) are actually a premium space in the kitchen because everyone uses them all the time.

The trick to keeping a junk drawer organized is to add containers for all the things that belong here. Use oblong containers for screwdrivers, pliers, scissors, and other small tools. Use small containers for stick pins, tacks, screws, keys, rubber bands, and tape. Ice cube trays make a good container for small things. This drawer is home to only things you use on a regular basis and you want right at your finger tips. Everything else is placed in the BE basket to be taken to its home after you finish here for the day.

Extra electrical cords or telephone cords can be secured with a rubber band or folded inside empty toilet paper rolls and placed in the hanging shoe organizer in the entryway closet or placed in a drawer that is not in the kitchen. Or cut the toe off a sock and fold cords up in the sock for storage.

Tip: Put all tape used in the home in one drawer (masking tape, duct tape, clear tape for wrapping gifts, and packing tape). Then, when you need any kind of tape, you know right where to find it. It is also good to have tape you use most often in the resource drawer.

Countertops

Countertops are premium spaces in many kitchens. Remove all the appliances you keep on the counters that you use only use once every six months. Refer to the section on bulky appliances (on page 79) for ideas on where to store them.

If your appliances are large and take up a lot of space, consider looking for smaller, streamlined appliances to keep on your countertops. They take up less space and have many combined functions (i.e., many rice cookers are also steamers, so you don't need two separate appliances, or get a toaster oven that is also a toaster). Many appliances (such as the microwave, toaster oven, television, radio, can opener, or paper towel holder) can be mounted under the overhead cupboards. If you have room, purchase a mini kitchen island on wheels. This will give you more counter space and storage space underneath as well.

If your mail gets tossed on the kitchen counter, put an attractive basket in the corner for it to land in. Or attach a mail holder on the wall. More will be discussed about mail in Chapter 11.

Refrigerator and Freezer

Remove everything from the refrigerator. Wash it out with baking soda to give it a fresh smell (two tablespoons of soda to about one pint of water). The important thing about organizing the refrigerator is to keep like items together: condiments on the door, milk and juices on the top shelf, yogurt, cottage cheese, and eggs on another shelf. Refrigerators have meat drawers and crisper bins for fruits and vegetables. Wash your fruits and vegetables before you put them in the refrigerator. Use these spaces for their intended uses. It keeps like items together and your refrigerator organized. Don't crowd the food in the refrigerator or freezer so tight that air can't circulate.

Store food in the refrigerator from 34–40°F (1–4°C). Food spoils rapidly above 40°F (3°C). The temperature in frostless and self-defrosting refrigerators is fairly uniform throughout the refrigerator; this includes the storage area on the door. If your refrigerator must be defrosted manually, the coldest area outside the freezing unit is the chill tray just below it. The area at the bottom is the warmest. The door area is usually several degrees higher than the rest of the refrigerator.

The temperature in the freezer should be 0°F (-18°C). Check the temperatures periodically. Appliance thermometers are the best way of knowing these temperatures and are generally inexpensive.

Once a week, take a look through your refrigerator and throw away any leftovers and toss any vegetables and fruits that are no longer edible.

To make fixing lunches easier, keep everything needed to pack a lunch in a container in the fridge. Bread, meats, cheese, lettuce in small bags and even the bottles of mayo, mustard, and so forth can be in one place to save time looking for lunch fixings. In a cupboard or in the pantry, place everything else that is needed to makes lunches in a basket; crackers, treats, bread, and plastic sacks can all be contained. In the rush of the morning, there are only two containers to grab.

The easiest way to organize the refrigerator and freezer is with containers. (It's always about containers isn't it?) Put the meat in a container, the vegetables in another container, and the fruits in another container. Boxes of TV dinners or other things that come in boxes can stack nicely by themselves, or place them in a container.

> **Tip:** Store an opened box of baking soda in your refrigerator and freezer to help eliminate odors. Replace it every three months. It may need replacing sooner if it loses its effectiveness and there are odors in the refrigerator. Date the box with a permanent marker to remind you when to replace it. Most refrigerator stains can be easily removed by cleaning with baking soda, and it leaves your refrigerator smelling fresh.

WRAP UP

There is a peace you feel when your kitchen is organized. Take a look at it now and compare it to the before photo. Wow! What a big difference. I am proud of you, and I know what a big difference this will make to you in your life.

You have successfully done these things in your kitchen, and these steps will help you keep it organized:

- You organized the inside of your cupboards! When you open your cupboards you feel joy. You might find yourself opening your cupboard doors just to look inside because they now have a bright feeling instead of being dark.
- You have reclaimed your counters. No more cooking surrounded by clutter. A basket for mail has solved the problem of mail all over the counter. Don't you feel great? You have accomplished a lot.

- Appliances have been put away, and you are only keeping what you use. You got rid of the ones you never used—goodbye guilt.
- It is easy to cook, set the table, and wash up because everything is easily accessible from cupboards to the table to the dishwasher and back into the cupboards again.
- The trash is contained, which makes a big difference in the look and feel in the room.
- You now have resource drawers instead of junk drawers.
- You labeled shelves in the pantry to make it easier to find things and put them away.
- The refrigerator and freezer are clean, and there is a place for everything you store there. (You may not eat out as much because you know what you will fix for dinner, and you'll save money.)

Doesn't it feel great to have an organized kitchen? Isn't it easier to prepare food and to cook without clutter? What a cheery place this is for you and your family to get together and have family time! Your kitchen will be a happy gathering place for everyone. Encourage family members to put things away where they belong after using them. This will be easy because the shelves are labeled.

Now your kitchen is efficient, and it feels like the heart of the home and a well-run nerve center. This is where everyone in the family comes first thing in the morning, and it is the last room they visit at night. Kids are taught how to cook here. They share their day's adventures over meals or while dinner is being prepared. Craft projects and homework are done at the kitchen table. Conversation between the adults while dinner is being prepared or around the dinner table happens in this room. Rate your wattage in this room. You are shooting for a 7 or above.

The Master Bedroom

(6)

Do you enjoy going into your master bedroom and snuggling deep down under the covers with a good book or with that special someone? Your bedroom is your personal, private sanctuary.

The master bedroom is the place to create a peaceful, restful space specifically for you in your home. It's the room you walk into at the end of the day, leaving the cares of the world behind you. It is a place where you can relax, connect, and bond with your significant other or just be alone. If it is cluttered, it makes it hard to relax and fall asleep. The clutter is another reminder that there are things that still need to be done. Let's create a sanctuary in the master bedroom—a place of retreat, free from clutter and chaos.

SEARCHLIGHT

Starting from the inside out, look in the closets, dressers, and nightstands. Then, working from left to right (like reading a book), look for things you like about this room and for things you don't like. Write them in your notebook. Can you feel and see what is keeping you from the highest wattage when you are in your bedroom? While you are looking around, take a picture so when you're finished you can look back and see what great improvements you have made. Be sure to take a picture of the inside of your closet—by the time you are finished, you will be amazed at the transformation! The closet is often the messiest and most frustrating place in the bedroom. We toss things in, and we grab things out, telling ourselves some day it will be different. Write your responses to the following questions in your notebook:

1. What is it you like about this room? What lights you up?
2. What don't you like about this room? Does it make you feel agitated and restless? Identify your needs by asking yourself the following questions:
   a. What type of atmosphere do you want in this room?
   b. Do you have a hard time falling asleep, and could this be because of the clutter and chaos?
   c. Is this room neglected?
   d. Is the closet functional?
   e. Can you find things you need on the nightstand?
   f. Is there too much furniture for the amount of space?
   g. Are the dressers organized and are the things that you need and use nice and tidy?
   h. Is the room a dumping ground with all flat surfaces, including the floor, piled with clutter and clothes?
   i. How did it get this way? What are you doing to keep it this way?
   j. Has it become a habit to just throw things in and shut the door because guests don't see this room?

Paula's Story

Can you relate to Paula, who dreaded taking her Searchlight and looking at her bedroom? She already knew she wasn't happy or lit up when she was in her bedroom, but she was determined to make some changes.

She liked the colors in her room, and she loved her big, soft comfy chair. She did wish she could use the chair for reading instead of a clothes hanger.

The bed was always covered with laundry that needed folding. Her nightstand was piled with old magazines, paper wrappers, and dirty dishes. Her closet was stuffed with clothes she hadn't worn in a year, that she didn't like, or that didn't fit. She had held on to the clothes thinking that "one day" she would fit in them again. (Haven't we all felt that way?) These clothes were discouraging to her, and she felt guilty for not being able to wear them. She decided that when she became the clothes size she wanted to be, she would reward herself and buy some new clothes instead of living in the past and hanging on! The dresser drawers looked like someone had taken an egg beater to the clothes; they were such a jumbled mess. She couldn't wait to light up this room to a 10!

> Get rid of clothes that are too small. When you reach your ideal size, reward yourself with new clothes.

Shut the World Out

I encourage you not to have a television or computer in your bedroom. These get in the way of creating a peaceful haven as they create a different focus. Catching up on the nightly news or answering just one more e-mail is inviting the outside world into your bedroom instead of using the time to connect by communicating, inviting intimacy and bonding or just having some quiet time by yourself to think or rest. The bedroom is a place to go to unwind and sleep after a long day.

    k. Are there things here that belong in other rooms (laundry, toys, craft projects)?

3. You have gone through the closets and nightstands, looked under the bed, behind the door, and in the dressers and rated everything. What is your wattage number now (see page 15)? When you are in this room, are you lit up at a 7 or above? If not, then you have some things to do.

Now that you have answered these questions and written down your answers, you can move on to using the Spotlight to set goals to make some changes.

SPOTLIGHT

By using the Searchlight, you know exactly what needs to be done. With the Spotlight, you are going to get right down to it and set some goals. As you accomplish each one, check it off.

Here are some examples of goals you could set:

1. This will be a sanctuary where you can relax and unwind.
2. Closet chaos will be conquered! The closet will hold only the clothes you

actually wear. Shelves will be organized; shoes, scarves, and belts will have a designated area. Wire and plastic hangers will be donated.

3. Nightstands will be functional both inside and out; no clutter will be allowed on the top.
4. All clothes will be kept off the floor and folded or hung where they belong.
5. Everything in this room will have a designated place where it will live.
6. Bed sheets will be changed regularly.
7. Pictures will be hung on the walls to give the room a warm, peaceful feeling.
8. Dresser tops will be free of clutter, including too many figurines or pictures.

Write down a target date to complete these goals. This will help you to stay focused and keep on track.

GREEN LIGHT

This is the most exciting part. You are going to see wonderful changes. Refer to your goals, and let's get going. Stay in the Green Light by wearing comfortable clothes. Gather your tool kit (see page 22) and your four containers (see page 35).

Get a drink (water is my favorite as it actually gives your body energy) and a snack. Set your timer for a specific amount of time. I recommend at least one hour. You want to get a lot done in a short period of time, and you can do it if you stick to it. Either take the phone off the hook or, if it rings, let the answering machine pick up and you can listen to the message when you take a break. (Schedule a time later in the day to check messages and return calls.)

When your timer rings, if you are engrossed in what you are doing, reset the timer and keep going! When you take a break, set your timer for five minutes so you will remember to come back and get your room organized.

Start working from the inside out. I bet one of your biggest headaches is your closet. So start there. You will create a big mess and chaos in this room before it is all back together and looking wonderful—but rest assured it will go from chaos to organized.

Places to start:

1. closet
2. dresser
3. nightstand
4. under the bed
5. other furniture (armoires, benches/chests)

Closet

Remove everything systematically from the closet. In case you don't finish today, you will want to be able to go to bed tonight, so you don't want to remove what is on the shelves, closet rod and floor all at the same time. Removing everything from the closet will take some time, but just think what surprises and hidden treasures you will find.

There is a reason for taking everything out of your closet. I know this is a big project, and everyone groans about it, so here is the logic behind removing everything:

1. You will be able to see exactly what kind of space you have to work with.
2. You will be astonished and maybe embarrassed by the pile of stuff now sitting on your floor, bed, couch, or the cat. This will give you the itch to organize it neatly and in a way that it is useful for you.

Start on the Floor: Remove everything from the closet floor. (Don't try to be sneaky and just leave that one little box there because you know what is in it.) Start on the floor so you'll have room to move in the closet. If the floor is piled with stuff, you won't be able to get into the closet. This is true for a walk-in closet or for a small closet.

Here are a few suggestions for what to put back on the floor: a clothes hamper (only if you must have one here); pull-out drawers that serve as a dresser if you don't have space in the room, and shoes (either on the floor or on a shoe rack).

Now that you have removed everything from the floor, start putting the shoes back in the closet. Look at each pair and ask yourself: do they still fit; do I like them; do they light me up; do I have clothes to wear them with; are they in need of repair or do they need polishing? If you answered no to any of the first four questions and they are in good condition, either donate them or throw them away. If they need repairing or polishing and you are keeping them, don't put them back in the closet yet. Place them in the BE basket. Get someone in your home to polish them for you. OK, if that doesn't work, you can do it later tonight while watching television. Take the ones that need fixing to your car (when you are unloading the BE basket, not right now).

If you store your shoes on the floor, I recommend placing them on a shoe rack. You can see your shoes more easily, and having a designated place to store them will take care of the problem of shoes being scattered everywhere. If your closet has wood shelves or cubby holes, shoes can be stored there. Shoe organizers that fit over the closet rod or those that fit over the door are great containers to use for shoes. Clear, plastic shoeboxes can hold shoes, keeping them free from dust and making them easy to see. It is your preference as to how you store your shoes.

Take a break, or at least take a breath, and a drink of water, and we'll move on to phase two in the closet.

Tip: Plastic shoeboxes can make perfect pull-out drawers for underwear, sweaters, shorts, jeans, or other clothing, and they can fit under hanging clothing.

Closet Rod: Take everything off the closet rod. If your closet is divided by his and hers, I recommend you do one side at a time. These instructions and ideas work for both sides.

I like to lay out a sheet on the bed to lay the clothes on that I remove from the closet. I know the clothes are clean, but I just like to protect nice quilts or duvets. As you take clothes out, keep likes together as much as you can (shirts, pants, skirts, belts, etc.). It will save you time when you start putting things back.

Now you can assess how much space you have in your closet. If you don't have enough shelving, suspend a hanging rack from the rod. There are canvas units that hang from the rod that can be used as drawers, which are useful for socks and underwear, sweaters, or scarves. Or suspend a hanging rod that hooks over existing rods. They are inexpensive and instantly create extra room for hanging short clothes. Shelf dividers that can be placed on the shelf above the rod can be used to prevent leaning towers of sweaters or other items stored there.

Tip: There is a good reason wire hangers are free: They are worthless. To increase the life and shape of your clothes, don't keep them on wire or flimsy plastic hangers. Wooden and padded hangers are the best kind to maintain the shape of a garment. A cotton-padded hanger helps prevent slinky shirts and camisoles from slipping off, and there is no risk of fabric snagging or ripping. The elongated hook and curved shoulders of a padded hanger provides support for shirts and suit jackets. For pants and skirt hangers, have some kind of fabric barrier to protect clothes from clamps.

Your closet is premium space, so only those clothes you like to wear, that fit you, and are in good repair should be using this space.

As you put your clothes back into the closet, look at each article and evaluate each item using these three criteria:

1. If you haven't worn it at least once in the last year, donate it. (Obviously you won't miss it.)
2. If you are hoarding clothes waiting for that weight to come off, *stop*— that is part of the reason your closet got into this mess to begin with. I

recommend only keeping clothes you can wear right now. If you must, only keep sizes one size larger or smaller than your present size. Move the smaller or larger clothes to a different space, either into another closet or fold and store them in labeled bins you place on a closet shelf or in the storage room or garage. Donating clothes will save you a lot of space, and when you get in shape again, you can buy new, stylish clothes.

3. Check each article to see if it is ripped, stained, missing a button, or has a zipper that doesn't zip. If it is completely unsalvageable, it goes into the throw-away container. However, do not throw it away just because you think it is ugly—those items go into your donate bin. Give as many things as you can to charity. You will be helping someone else. It will make you feel good. It will create space in your closet, and you may get a tax deduction.

After you finish this process, you should have fewer clothes than when you started. If you don't, then the laws of physics apparently do not apply to your closet. You will now divide the clothing into three categories. This is the fun part of closet organizing.

1. *The Season Category* (unless you live where there is only one season): If it is an off-season article, put it with your seasonal clothes. Either fold and store them in labeled bins on a closet shelf or hang them in another closet. If you don't have other closet space, store seasonal clothes in the back of your closet.

2. *The Type Category:* Arrange all blouses together by long sleeve, short sleeve, and color or by casual (T-shirts), dressy (church), sweaters, and hoodies. Place all skirts together, separated by length; hang dresses all together, all suits together and then sport coats, slacks, and dressy pants. Hang all clothes facing the same direction and have the hangers all facing the same way (the hook facing the wall). You can sort by

Make the Most of Closet Space

Cece lived in a one-bedroom condo that did not have any storage space, and she didn't have a dresser. She added a wire shelf on top of the existing shelf in the closet because there was a lot of unused vertical space above the shelf that she could use for storage.

She divided her closet shelf into sections using shelf dividers. In one section on the top shelf, she stored extra sheet sets. In another area, she stored holiday dishes (in a labeled container), seasonal sport clothes, and reference magazines placed in attractive magazine holders. This is the shelf she used for things she needed to keep, but didn't use often. This shelf was her secondary space.

On the bottom shelf, she stored hand and bath towels, pants, T-shirts, and anything else she would normally keep in a dresser.

arranging professional clothes together, including any outfits you might wear on office-casual days. This will make getting dressed so easy you can push your snooze button one extra time in the morning. Separate your special occasion outfits and hang them together. By now, you have gotten rid of your junior prom dress (at the very least you have moved it to a different closet), so returning the clothes to the closet should be pretty easy to manage. Organize casual clothes together. These include your weekend wear that only your cat should see you in.

3. *The What-on-Earth-Is-This Category:* You have all the clothes you love and wear neatly arranged in the closet, but you are left with a pile of odds and ends we will call "accessories." They are a mixture of belts,

scarves, suspenders, and ties. Hang the ties from a rack made for ties. The belts and suspenders can be hung from a hook or a special rack for belts. They can also all be hung together using a hanger. If you use them often, this is a pain as you have to take off each belt to get to the other ones, but it is another option. Scarves can be folded in a drawer or hung up using a scarf organizer.

If you keep purses in your closet, here are some storage ideas: Place them in a basket and store it on the top shelf. If you have a walk-in closet, place them in a basket and store it on the built-in shelves. An over-the-door purse organizer with adjustable hooks for each purse size makes it easy for you to see what purses you have and makes them easy to reach. Another option is to install a hook to hang purses from. Decorative hooks can be attached to a wall behind the bedroom door if you don't have a walk-in closet.

Tip: After you have worn an article of clothing and you are hanging it back on the rod, place it on the rod backwards (with the hook facing forward) so you can tell which clothes you actually wear. If you find you have clothes that you never wear, donate them.

Top Shelf: To start, take everything off the shelf. Get a short ladder, step stool, or chair to stand on so you don't pull a muscle trying to get things down.

The top shelf is space you use for items you don't have room for in other places in your home if you have limited space elsewhere. Use containers to keep this area organized. Types of containers to use are: sturdy mesh, plastic, canvas, or cloth boxes and shelf dividers with sides used to contain stacks. You can use various sizes depending on what you are storing on the shelf.

In a small home, in addition to clothes, closet shelves can hold containers of CDs, jewelry, games, magazines in holders, gifts to give away, or craft supplies.

The key to organizing the closet shelf is to use containers that are attractive and that fit on the shelf. Organize so things don't fall on your head when you open the door. Make it an attractive part of your closet.

Dresser

Take everything out one drawer at a time. Wipe out the drawer. It is surprising what stuff falls in there. I recommend organizing one side of a his-and-hers dresser at a time, not going back and forth. Keep in mind, you are going to go to bed tonight without tossing anything from the bed onto the floor. If you get out a lot of things all at once, it could be too overwhelming. That is the reason I recommend doing one drawer at a time.

Start with the top drawer and take everything out. Put containers in the drawer to hold lingerie or socks. Clear plastic ones are my favorite because they can't be seen, and it looks mysterious to see everything staying in their respective stacks.

Inspect everything you put back in the drawer (i.e., Does it fit? Do you like it? Is it in good condition? Do you give it a 7 or above on the wattage scale?). If you answered "no" to any of these questions, get rid of it or get it fixed before you put it back in the drawer if you want to keep it. (Put it in the BE basket.)

Once the top drawer is organized, systemically move down to the other drawers and organize these in the same way, keeping like things together and using containers. Or, if your dresser has a lot of smaller drawers, organize all the top ones and then move down to the larger ones. Fold each item and place it in its home. If your sock drawer is out of control, a sock container where you can toss your socks is one way to contain them. These containers also work for underwear, or underwear can just be folded and placed in stacks.

Now clean off the top of the dresser. Put things that don't belong here in the BE basket or the trash, or donate items you are not keeping. Some things to keep on the dresser could be framed photos, a jewelry box or a jewelry tree, a special figurine, a container for change, and your wallet.

Nightstand

The top of the nightstand next to the bed is used to hold a lamp, phone, alarm clock, and other things such as books, tissues, and possibly a remote control.

When you think of a nightstand, do you think of the traditional small piece of furniture that sits demurely by your bed? Nightstands don't have to be limited to this type of furniture.

If you love to read and have books galore on your nightstand and the books are always falling onto the floor, maybe a small bookcase would work better for you. You could stack your books on the shelves and still have room for a lamp and other items you need close to your bed. Things you would usually keep in a bedside drawer can be kept in a storage box or wicker basket that sits on a shelf.

Are you short of space in your bedroom? A chest of drawers next to the bed could hold a lamp and other items. Tissues, books, and hand lotion could slip into the top drawer. Additional drawers can hold clothing, bed linens, blankets, or towels.

Another type of nightstand is a round table with a tablecloth on it. Only keep things on top that are useful. Store other items you need in a basket and put it under the table where it will be handy but out of sight.

Whatever kind of nightstand you have right now, if there are drawers, take everything out and decide if these things belong in these drawers. Ask yourself if you have a use for the item, if you like it, and if it lights you up at a 7 or above. Only put back things that fit that criteria.

To organize your nightstand, set your timer for fifteen minutes and play beat the clock. I bet you will be done before the fifteen minutes are over—or close to it. Reset the timer if you need more time.

Under the Bed

Take everything out from under the bed. Look at each thing you pull out and decide if you want to keep it or get rid of it. Use the wattage scale (see page 15) to help you decide. Use the BE basket when you find things like dishes, books, or toys; do not leave the room yet, stay in the Green Light.

If you need to store things under the bed, there are cloth containers for out-of-season clothes, extra quilts, extra bed linens, and other items you may need to store in this space. Other containers that fit under beds are plastic and have rollers. This makes them easy to access as they slide in and out easily.

Other Furniture

Armoires are useful for holding extra linens or quilts and even serving as a place to put clothes that traditionally are kept in dressers. Take everything out, wipe out the shelves and drawers, and refold whatever is to be returned (it weakens cloth to be folded in the same place for a long period of time). Only put back those things you have a use for and that light you up. If you use this as a dresser, containers could give you more space and keep things tidy.

If you use an armoire for an entertainment center, take out everything that doesn't belong there and then dust the shelves and electronic equipment. Put things that don't belong there in the BE basket.

Benches or chests are great containers for quilts, sheets, and off-season clothes. Take everything out, even if you think you know what is in there. It will remind you of what you have, and you can refold the items. Donate any items you no longer like or want to keep. Giving things to others is a good thing. Please don't feel guilty for letting go, especially if someone else has given it to you. There is no rule that says you have to keep it. A chest is either storage space for you or it is a secondary storage area. If you get into the chest at least once a month, make it convenient to do so.

If a good friend or relative has given you something and you are keeping it just because they gave it to you, go ahead and bless someone else's life by donating it to charity. If you have too many of anything, or you don't like something, let go of it. The peace you will feel and the mind-clearing experience will be worth it.

WRAP UP

You have done it! Your bedroom is now a 10. The closet is organized from the floor to the top shelf. Dressers, nightstands, and under the bed are clutter-free.

Let your family know this is your own private sanctuary, and it is not a play room for the kids or a dumping ground for stuff from other parts of the home. It is not a laundry room, so the laundry does not live in this room. The ironing board is also not allowed here. We will talk about laundry in Chapter 13. Going to bed will be something you'll look forward to; with the room free of clutter, you will probably sleep better. It will be more fun when your little kiddies come in to snuggle in bed and your teenage children come to talk.

You have accomplished a lot, and your bedroom can stay organized because:

- The closet only holds clothes you can wear. Off-season clothes are in a secondary space. It will take less time to dress when going out because clothes are not crowded. Shoes have a designated place to be stored, and the closet shelf is being used to its capacity.
- The dresser is organized so you can readily find your clothes, and lingerie and socks are contained.
- The nightstand is functional with only a minimal amount of things on the surface. Other items are in the drawer with containers for smaller items.
- You know what is under the bed, and items are stored in containers to keep them dust free and organized.
- Armoires or benches/chests have been inspected, and you are keeping only what you want.

Congratulations on a great job! Give yourself a pat on the back, or you can even lie down and take a nap in your peaceful bedroom.

7 Children's Bedrooms

You've heard the saying, "Actions speak louder than words." Expecting children to have their rooms organized while the rest of the home is unorganized will never work. Children learn by example.

Often children's bedrooms are messy, and the children get the blame when it might not be entirely their fault. Kids can't keep their rooms straight if they don't have homes for their toys, clothes, art supplies, and other treasures. It is up to the parent or caregiver to come up with storage solutions and guidance for the children. It is interesting how children can be reared in the same home and yet they have very different organizing skills. Sometimes, we just have to embrace the differences and come up with individual systems for each child that will help him or her organize.

It May Take Some Time

My friend's teenage daughter "liked" her room messy—meaning things were all over the floor, dresser, and nightstand. There was a lot of conflict between my friend and her daughter about her room always being a mess. They finally came to an agreement that the daughter would keep her door closed so her mother couldn't see all the clutter. Her daughter agreed to clean her room and put her clothes and other things away once a week. The daughter has now graduated from college and is living in an apartment of her own. She is neat, tidy, and organized. (In fact, she complains that her housemates aren't organized.)

Sometimes children just have to grow up to become organized. Teaching and encouraging them when they are young will help them both while they are at home and after they have moved to their own place. (With some children, it just takes longer to see the results of your teaching.)

SEARCHLIGHT

How you look at this room will depend on the age of the child. If you are transitioning the child's room from a baby's nursery, where you are responsible for how it looks, to a child's room, it will be different than organizing for a child who is older. Before you start organizing the room, always get the child's input, permission, and participation if the child is old enough. Do not surprise an older child by organizing his or her room without permission as privacy and personal belongings need to be respected.

If they tell you to "Just do it yourself!" do not accept this invitation for the following reasons: When they have an interest in a project and have a sense of ownership and responsibility your children will be more likely to have pride in what is done; and when organizing their room, they will want to keep it organized by keeping things in their places. Organization is a necessary life skill that many adults have not been taught, and this is a great teaching moment in your child's life. It is part of your child's early education. The advantages of teaching them to organize their rooms when they are young starts with small things, and as they mature, they move on to accepting more responsibility, from putting toys away, picking up books, and hanging up their clothes to being responsible to do their own laundry.

> "Sandwich every bit of criticism between two layers of praise."
>
> –MARY KAY ASH

Use the Searchlight to look for things that are working for your child and for you. Write these things in your notebook to show your children you are interested in them and are willing to use your time to help them organize their bedrooms. It will be their sanctuaries for their personal time alone or time with friends. Take a picture so you can have a before and after view.

1. What do you and your child like about this room?
2. What don't you both like about this room? To help you identify needs ask yourself the following questions:
    a. What things besides clothes have to be in this room (books, toys, games, etc.)?
    b. Is this room for sleeping and reading only or is it also a play room?
    c. Are there places to store the things the child needs in the room? Do you have shelves for books, toys, and collections? Do you have containers for toys?

    d. Is there too much stuff for the amount of space?

    e. Is your child always saying "Mom where is....," or "I can't find my homework," etc.?

    f. Is this room kid-friendly? Are closet rods, drawers, and containers within easy reach for them? Can they easily put their clothes and toys away?

    g. Are there different areas in the room, such as a play area, a sleeping area or a creative area?

3. Ask your child what his or her wattage is in this room (see page 15). Ask him or her what you can do to improve that wattage.

Tip: *If there is one room in your home that is a war zone, I bet it is your child's bedroom. Is it a jumbled mess of clothes, toys, papers, and books? When parents yell, "Clean your room!" it means one thing to the child and another to the parent. Clear expectations and good communication are two important factors to bringing peace and ending misery for both the child and the parents.*

SPOTLIGHT

You have decided what you need and want to change in this room. Now with your Spotlight, you can set goals and create the kind of room you and your child would like to have. Here are some examples of goals you could set for this room:

1. The bed will be made every morning.

2. Shelves and rods will be within easy reach for the child to put away clothes that belong in the closet.

3. There will be a designated area for every item kept in the closet. Shelves, hooks, and rods will be labeled to make putting things away easy for the child.

4. Dresser drawers will be labeled (if necessary, depending on the child's

Paula's Story

Paula was ready to use the Spotlight in her eight-year-old son's room. She and her son set the following goals: Lower the closet rod so he can reach it. Sort through all the clothes to see if he could still use them and check to see if they needed mending. Put a basket on the floor for him to toss his shoes in (she knew he would never line them up on a shoe rack). Remove all sports equipment and place it in a more convenient location in the family entryway.

In the drawers, she would add containers for socks, underwear, T-shirts, and sport clothes. She would show him where the clothes were to go in each drawer. She would check his room every day and watch him put away his clean clothes in the drawers until the habit was formed. She would give him a small box to use to store his "treasures." Toys were taking over the room. She would pare down the toys and place them in one basket with a lid. This was the amount of toys allowed in his bedroom.

> Come up with solutions that your children will be able to follow on a consistent basis.

She would purchase a bulletin board made of cork, and he could pin his artwork on the board. She established the rule that when a new piece of art goes up an old one comes down to be recycled or put in his school-year envelope. She wrote down her goals and felt confident they would be accomplished as she discussed each one with her son and got his input and approval.

age), and dividers or containers will make it easy for him or her to put clothing where it belongs.

5. There will be places and containers for toys to be contained.
6. Books will be organized in a specific place.
7. Craft supplies will be organized and contained in a designated area.
8. There will be a place for the child's artwork.

These principles will help you organize your child's room and help the child keep the room organized:

- Have a home for everything. (Remember the saying, a place for everything and everything in its place.)
- Have containers to keep things in.
- Don't cram the closet and dresser full of clothes. If there are too many clothes, remove some. Keep only a reasonable amount of clothing and make sure it's clothing currently being worn. (Put out-of-season clothes in storage.)
- Don't cram the room full of toys. Fewer toys opens up space in containers and makes it easier to put things away.

It will be easier to organize if you provide the child with everything needed to be organized. If you need to purchase any shelves or containers for the room, do so now. Measure areas where you plan to use containers so you purchase the correct sizes. Also measure all areas where you plan to place shelving units (whether it's a bookcase or simple cubbies or shelves). Make sure everything will fit in the room before you bring it into your home. Record a target date to accomplish these goals.

GREEN LIGHT

Now that you and your child have taken a good look at his or her bedroom and your goals are set, you have the Green Light to take action. Schedule a time with your child to get going. Set your timer for twenty minutes. You will want to work much more than this, but you can make a game out of organizing by seeing how much you both can get done in twenty minutes. Children's attention spans are shorter than adult's, so your child may not be able to keep working as long as you can, but start and finish with him or her, getting his or her input as you go. Get a drink, a snack, your tool kit (see page 22) and your four containers (see page 35).

Start this project when your child is energetic and rested. As with all rooms, start organizing from the inside out. Here's the order I suggest you work in:

1. closet
2. dresser
3. toys
4. bookshelves (or any other shelving unit outside of the closet)
5. desk
6. under the bed
7. artwork
8. treasures

Closet

Tackle the closet in sections so you don't get into a project you can't finish in one organizing session. Start with the floor, then the rod, then the shelves.

> **Tip:** *If the closet has sliding doors that always come off the track or make it hard to access parts of the closet, consider taking the doors off and storing them in the garage until the child is older and it is easier for him or her to reach the middle of the closet. You can cover the closet with a curtain rod and floor-length curtains instead of a door.*

Closet Floor: Have your child help by clearing out everything on the floor. Sort everything on the floor into one of the four bins (trash, recycle, donate, or BE). Evaluate each item left over. It should belong in the child's room, but does the item belong on the closet floor? If it does, create a home for it on the closet floor. If it belongs somewhere else in the room, put it in a pile to be put away later.

Now that everything is off the closet floor, what should the floor be used for?

- Shoes. Put a shoe rack on the floor or a small shelf or bookcase. Or use a shoe organizer that hangs from the closet rod or the door. Or you can install shelves at the ends of the closet and place shoes on the shelves. You can also use these shelves for folded clothes as well. Evaluate all shoes before you put them back in the closet. They must fit and be in good condition if you keep them. Hand-me-down shoes for another child belong in the BE basket. Place them in that child's room later or in a designated storage area.

- Clothes cubbies. If your child's room is small, make more space by leaving a dresser out of the room. Place plastic bins (cubbies) for clothes on the closet floor or put a dresser in the closet if there is room. Clothes can be separated by type: shirts in one cubby, pants in another, socks in another, and underwear in another. Or rolling carts that have wire baskets, or those with plastic drawers, can hold clothes. These are portable and lightweight.

- Storage containers for toys. Use slide-out plastic drawers stacked on top of each other.
- Laundry basket. Place a laundry basket on the closet floor or hang one from a hook or closet rod. There are cloth and net bags that also work well. Keep it easy and convenient for your child to use. Give the child the responsibility to take his or her laundry to the laundry room. More will be discussed about children's laundry in Chapter 13.

Tip: *Be creative. Above the laundry or waste basket install a small basketball hoop (the kind that comes with a suction cup to attach to the wall or hang over a door). This is a fun way to encourage kids to put their clothes in the laundry or trash in the waste basket.*

Closet Rod: Take all clothes off the closet rod. The rods should be placed at a height the child can easily reach. Organize likes together: shirts, pants, dresses, blouses, and skirts. Clothes will hang nicer and the closet will look better if you use all the same type of hangers. It is OK to use plastic hangers for children's clothes as they aren't as heavy and will hang fine on plastic, but avoid thin wire hangers for the clothes.

Have your child try on any infrequently worn clothes to see if they fit. Only replace clothes that do fit and are worn frequently. Does your child have too many clothes? This might be the reason the clothes are all over the floor and there is laundry everywhere. Paring down the amount of clothing your child has will help the child keep his or her clothes put away, and you'll have less clothes to launder.

Put the other clothes in the donate bin if they are still in good condition or in the BE basket if they will be hand-me-downs for another sibling, or in the trash if they cannot be donated.

Closet Shelves: Take everything off all of the shelves in the closet. If you need more storage space on the top shelf where there is wasted vertical space, add wire racks that can be purchased at your local home store or discount store.

Out-of-season clothes can be folded and placed in labeled plastic bins and stored on the top shelf. Clothes that are too large for the child can also be stored here in the same way. I do not recommend storing toys in clear bins on the shelf as curious children will often climb to reach them. If you do store toys here, put them in colored plastic bins. Label the containers so you will know what is in them. You also can store seasonal sports gear on the top shelf.

Use open bins when storing items on lower shelves for kids. They can see the toys, games, or other items, and it will be easy for them to reach and to put away.

Labeling shelves helps children know where things are to be stored. If they are too young to read, tape pictures on the edge of the shelf.

Tip: *If you have the closet designed specifically for your child's height, be sure it can grow with him or her. The rods, shelves, and other storage features should be adjustable so you can modify them as your child grows.*

Dresser

Take everything out of the dresser drawers. Chances are that every drawer has items in it that belong in other drawers. Have the child wipe out the drawers with a damp cloth. Sort all of the clothing by putting likes together: underwear, socks, pajamas, pants, and shirts. Designate one drawer or half of a drawer for each type of clothes. You may want to label the drawers inside or on the edge of the front so your child will know where to put his or her clothes. Dividers or containers inside drawers help keep clothes in their designated places. Look at all the clothes as you put them back and check that they fit the child, that the child likes the clothes, and that the child actually wears the clothing items.

The top of the dresser can be a clutter magnet. Some things that could be kept

Teach Children Generosity

Twice a year, Tammy and her husband had their children gather up toys and stuffed animals they didn't play with anymore. They had a family night where they cleaned the toys and washed the faces of the stuffed animals or dolls (including the clothes if necessary) and took them to a local family shelter. Their kids looked forward to this activity. It taught them about kindness and giving and also reduced clutter in their bedrooms.

there are a basket that holds diapers (if it's a baby's room), a family picture, trophies or special awards, a small jewelry box, a souvenir from a trip, and a lamp.

I do not recommend putting storage baskets on top of the dresser because little children may try to climb up and pull on them to see what is in them, and they could hurt themselves. Having too many things on top of dressers makes the room look cluttered.

Toys

One key to keeping toys organized is having homes for all of the toys. That means having enough containers to handle all types and sizes of the toys.

Small Toys and Puzzles: To store puzzles, put a symbol or the same number on the back of each piece for a specific puzzle. If puzzles get mixed up, you can easily separate them by matching the symbols or numbers. Storing them in a sealed plastic bag within the box keeps the pieces together even if the box gets tipped over (just be aware of the choking hazard bags pose). Games can be stored in Game Savers containers and placed on a shelf. I recommend a different room than the children's room to store puzzles and games. Designate a closet or storage container elsewhere in your home for these items. Building blocks and other small toys can be stored in ice cream tubs. Keep like toys together and label everything.

A shoe organizer can also hold small games and puzzles as well as craft items if these items are kept in the child's rooms. Label each pocket to keep them from becoming a catchall and to make it easy for the children to know where to return them after play.

Large Toys: Toy boxes and large plastic bins work great for storing large toys. If you use boxes and bins with lids, the lids automatically limit the amount of toys in the room. Use bins that stack on top of each other and separate toys by type. These bins can be kept in the closet to free up space in the room.

Stuffed Animals: There are mesh nets you can attach in the corner of a wall that function like a hammock, and you can put stuffed animals there. They can also be set on shelves that line the walls or hung from a floor-to-ceiling tension pole or from chain clips that are anchored from the ceiling.

Another key to keeping toys organized is to control the number of toys your child has. Set a number that is realistic for the size of your home and storage areas. One way to maintain this number is to donate an older toy each time a new toy enters your home. If you absolutely can't follow this "rule," store half of the toys and rotate them in and out of the toy box or toy baskets.

Every six to eight months, take an inventory of the toys. If the child has outgrown a toy or doesn't play with it anymore, it is time to donate it. Decide what to get rid of according to what the child plays with and likes, not according to who gave it to them, how much they once played with it, or how cute you think it is. You can donate toys to women's shelters or church groups, or swap toys with friends. If you have other children who may want the toy someday, put it in storage until the other child is old enough for the toy.

If you keep children's toys and other play things in their bedrooms, there are several things you can do to help keep them from becoming just more clutter.

- Rotate toys in and out of the toy box. This will make it seem like the child has more toys, and it is like having new ones when toys are swapped in and out. Toys not being used can be stored in covered bins in the closet.
- Divide all the toys evenly between seven different boxes. Label these boxes with days of the week. Say it is a Monday. Take down the box marked "Monday" and let the children play with the toys that are in that day's box. At the end of the day, the kids put away the toys and tomorrow they play with a completely different set of toys from the "Tuesday" box. On the days they are home all day and can't play outside because of the weather, rotate these boxes every few hours. They will have variety and won't get bored.

Tip: If toys and play things are kept in the family room or in a toy room, the same principles apply. Keep the toys contained in bins, cubbies, boxes, or some kind of sturdy containers. Clear plastic containers or open baskets are what I recommend because it is easy to see at a glance what is in them.

Bookshelves

Take everything off of bookshelves and wipe the shelves clean. Bookcases or freestanding shelves secured to the wall can hold not only books but many other things. Bins or baskets can hold children's craft supplies, puzzles, and collections if these are kept in the bedroom. Containers with lids are nice for pens, colored pencils, beads, and other craft items. An open basket can hold colored or plain paper as well as books. These can be placed on the bookshelves to make it convenient for children to use.

As you place books back on the shelf, make sure the books are age-appropriate and in good condition. Mend well-worn books that are family favorites. If the books have been scribbled in and can't be read, recycle them. Donate books that are no longer read or put them in the BE basket if you are going to put them in another place in your home (storing them for other children or putting them in other bookcases). If your child is an avid reader, get a library card and make the most of it. The library will expose the child to countless titles without cluttering your house or costing you money. When he or she finds a book that is a favorite, then you can buy that book.

> The library will expose your child to countless books without the clutter.

Desk

As your child gets older, a desk may be a nice addition to his or her room. It can hold school papers, and homework can be done there. For girls, it could double as a vanity where they can keep their fingernail polish, cosmetics, hair supplies, and makeup if the bathroom is too small to hold these things. Keeping these things in baskets makes it easy to carry them to the bathroom to use.

Under the Bed

It is hand-and-knees time. You may even need a broom to reach the far corner for that last lost sock or runaway toy. Sort everything you find here and put the items in their proper homes. If you store things under here, I recommend using the plastic containers with rollers; they are easy to pull out and they make the things in the containers easily accessible. Plastic bed risers or bed lifters will raise the bed about six to eight inches (15–20cm) off the floor and make more room for under-bed storage. The risers are sturdy and last for years.

You will probably be the only one accessing things stored under the bed, so don't keep frequently used items here. Encourage your children to clean under the bed as far as they can reach every time they clean their rooms so it doesn't become a clutter haven.

Displaying Your Child's Art

Here are some options for using and displaying the art your child creates. Rotate what's on display frequently and archive items or dispose of them if you find you no longer want to keep them.

- The refrigerator: As a professional organizer and mother this is my least favorite place for artwork as it creates clutter in the kitchen. However, if you like that look, then do it. But there are other wonderful options.
- Pin the art to a cork board or bulletin board.

- String a clothesline along one big wall in the child's bedroom and use clothespins to display the "collection" so it's like a gallery.
- Display it in an inexpensive poster-sized picture frame. A frame can hold one large piece or several smaller works.
- Attach strips of felt to a dowel rod and allow kids to pin their artwork directly to the felt.
- Use laminated artwork as placemats. You can give these to relatives or use them during meals or messy arts-and-crafts projects at home.
- Send artwork to relatives and let the child use the back to write letters on it.
- Use it for wrapping paper. If you intend to use it this way, put it with the wrapping paper, not just in a pile somewhere.

Artwork

Let me just say at the beginning, do not keep all of your children's art/school work! Just think, if you save everything your child brings home, by the time he or she is in college you will have a two-car garage over flowing with just the paperwork, and it will be spilling into your home. (I actually read about a woman who had saved every piece of paper, and this was the result.)

> **Tip:** *Encourage your children to play with or use their clay creations (after you have photographed them). Clay creations tend to break, and when that happens, you can dispose of the item and avoid the dilemma of what to do with it. These items will also become less important to the child as time goes on.*

A very wise preschool teacher passed on this little gem: Young children are into process, not product. Children live in the moment; they enjoy the moment of making the art but are quite casual about disposing of it. I have daughters, and as I have experienced this with them, I know this is true. So don't worry about hurting your child's feelings when you dispose of his or her latest creation. Unless he or she is very attached to the project, your child won't care.

Teaching your children what to keep and what to let go of now will help them when they are adults and dealing with their own paperwork. It's not just about their art or schoolwork—it's about how they (and you) approach organization.

When your child brings home artwork, graded papers and tests, and mementos, look at it and discuss it with him or her right away. Decide immediately what you will keep and what you will get rid of. Set reasonable limits, not just for your child but also for yourself. Then create a home for the "keepers" and place them there right away.

One option for saving paperwork is to use a large envelope—10½" × 15" (27cm × 38cm) is a good size. Write the child's name and age, the name of the school, the year in school (e.g., fifth grade), the school year (e.g., 2010–2011), and the teacher's name on the outside. (You can also do this for home-schooled children.) When they have school pictures taken, if you have extras tape one with clear packing tape to the front of the envelope. Have one envelope for each year your child is in school. Each child has his or her own envelope and own box. I recommend saving a sampling of school work, not just the best, but some that is "average." By saving a range of papers, it gives the child a view of what his or her school years were like. It is a truer look at what he or she did in school. As long as you follow the one-envelope limit, you can keep whatever sort of papers you want. At the end of the summer of that year (assuming he or she does some projects you want to keep from summer programs), place the envelope in storage by putting it in a container with a lid on it, such as an apple box, a copy paper box, or a purchased plastic bin. A good place to keep this box is on the top shelf of the child's closet. Decorate the box and label it with the child's name. I prefer using a plastic container with a lid.

If the artwork that comes into the house is bigger than your designated storage space, or it begins to pile up quicker than you can process it, take a picture of it with your child holding it. What a fun memory to look back on. Buy a photo album and create an "art album" for each child.

> Tip: Paper deteriorates over time. Storing paper in acid- and lignin-free containers will slow down the deterioration process, but you don't need this level of archive storage for your children's artwork and school papers. These materials are made of low-quality acidic paper so what does it matter if they are surrounded by acid-free covers. If you're concerned about the longevity of the pieces you've saved, you can photocopy them on acid- and lignin-free paper or photograph them for posterity.

Treasures

All children from a young age have treasures they want to keep: rocks, buttons, things they find or make, etc. Give your child a shoebox or a small plastic container and let him or her decorate it. Then let the child fill it up with his or her treasures. If the box gets too full, the child will need to get rid of some of the items to make room for new items. The child only get one "treasures" box each. Children's interests change quickly, so it shouldn't be hard for them to part with old things to make room for new. This keeps the child's treasures (what we see as junk) contained, and he or she is in charge of deciding what to keep without it being scattered all over the floor.

Get the Child Involved

To maintain the organization you and your child have done, each night before bed take five minutes and have the child put away anything he or she got out or wore that day. When the child is young, make a game of it by counting the items as he or she picks them up. Or set the timer for five minutes and play "beat the clock."

If your child doesn't know how to change sheets and make a bed and he or she is old enough to do this, schedule a time when you will teach him or her this skill. Place a responsibility chart in the room and put a star by each job completed: making the bed, picking up toys, hanging up clothes, picking up paperwork, etc. Reward your child with a new book or toy once he or she has a certain amount of stickers on the job chart—something small that will help encourage your child to continue keeping the room clean and organized.

WRAP UP

You did a great job! By working with your children, you have encouraged and taught them the fundamentals of organizing. Praise them for the efforts they make in keeping their rooms organized. Praise your children when they can find their things without searching all over the house for them or constantly asking you where something is.

Congratulations on:

- Following the goals you set.

- Teaching/encouraging your child to make his or her bed every day.
- Installing rods and shelves at the child's level.
- Assigning places for toys, artwork, books and craft supplies and making it easy to maintain by having containers for everything.
- Establishing a bedtime routine of tidying the room every night.
- Donating toys, clothes and books that your child no longer needs or uses, creating space and ending clutter, making it easier for your child to keep his or her room organized.
- Taking care of your child's artwork and involving him or her in this process and providing envelopes and a storage box.
- Creating a happy, cozy place for the child to sleep and to play.

These steps will keep your children's bedrooms organized. (Or at least give them a better chance at staying organized!)

8 Linen Closets

It is a good feeling to open your linen closet and see at a glance what is in there. Sheets are folded and placed on their own shelf. The shelves are labeled as to the size of sheets so they are easy to find without undoing them to determine which bed they will fit. The towels are divided and stacked by size.

If other things, such as personal items, are stored in this closet, they are kept in separate containers with lids. The containers can be stacked and labeled making it easy to find anything you are looking for. First aid supplies and medicines can be kept in separate containers and stored in this closet as well.

When your linen closet is organized, you will want your guests to help themselves to the towels just so they can see how nice it looks.

SEARCHLIGHT

This is not meant to be a catchall closet. Stand back and look at what your closet looks like. Take a photo of the interior of the closet. In your notebook write down what is working for you and what is not working. What problems are keeping you from the wattage you want when you use this closet?

1. What do you like about this space?
2. What don't you like about this space? Identify needs by asking the following questions:
   a. Are the sheets and towels jumbled together?
   b. Are the different sizes of sheets easy to identify?
   c. If you store more than linens here, are the other items in containers?
   d. Are there items that don't belong here?
   e. Can you see everything at a glance and find exactly what you need?
3. You have assessed what needs to be changed. Now rate the wattage you feel when you look in the closet by using the wattage scale (see page 15). Is this closet a 7 or higher to you?

SPOTLIGHT

You identified the problem areas in your linen closet, and now with the Spotlight you can focus on setting goals to make this closet more functional for you and your family. Here are examples of goals you could set for this closet:

1. Sheets will be folded and identified by size.
2. The closet will only be used for linens and extra personal items.
3. Excluding linens, all other things will be in containers.
4. Shelves and containers will be labeled.
5. Towels will be folded neatly by size and placed in stacks by type (e.g., bath, hand, washcloth).

Paula's Story

Have you ever felt like Paula did when she opened the door to her linen closet? She liked the color of her towels and that they were large and soft. She didn't like other things she saw. The sheets were rolled up haphazardly and shoved on the shelf with the towels. The towels were wadded up and stuffed on several different shelves and often fell out on the floor.

She kept extra personal items like toothpaste, toothbrushes, hair clips, lip gloss, and nail polishes here, and they were hard to find underneath everything else in the closet. She also kept medicines on a turntable but she had no idea if they were expired and didn't know what medicines she had.

Paula didn't like what she saw; she groaned and felt discouraged every time she needed to use things in this closet. She resolved to make changes and make this closet a 10.

GREEN LIGHT

This is the exciting part. With your goals in mind, use the Green Light and go organize. Getting this closet in order is just this simple—sort, fold, and stack.

Get your feet planted in the Green Light, put on your comfortable clothes, and round up your tool kit (see page 22) and your four containers (see page 35).

Schedule a time to whip this closet into shape. Set your timer for one hour. If it is a small closet, this will probably be enough time to organize every shelf.

Get your drink and a snack. You may not need a snack this time because this will go fast, but what a great excuse to have some chocolate.

Take everything out of the closet, clear off every shelf, and sort everything into categories: sheets (by size), towels (by size), dinner napkins, tablecloths, table runners, pillows, blankets, and off-season items. I lay down a sheet to place these items on so they won't get dirty being on the floor. In another area, put all the other "stuff."

Wipe every shelf clean. When putting things back, keep in mind premium, secondary, and semi-storage areas to determine where to put the items in the closet (see page 24). Put items you use daily, such as towels, in the premium space—at eye level and towards the front of the shelf. Make small stacks—you don't want the Leaning Tower of Pisa in your closet—or use closet organizers that allow you to make taller stacks if there is room. Separate piles by type—bath towels, hand towels, washcloths, etc. Label the edge of the shelves so everyone who uses this closet will know where things are stored.

Consider limiting the amount of sheets and towels you keep. Three sets of sheets per bed and three sets of bath towels, hand towels, and washcloths per person (remember guests will need towels, too) may be enough.

Tip: *Teach your family how to fold the towels so this task is done the same way by everyone and the towels will fit on the shelves. There is no right or wrong way to fold, but one common way to fold a towel is to fold it in half lengthwise, then in half again; then fold in thirds starting at one end.*

Look at everything before you put it back in the closet. Either toss old, thin, worn out towels or cut them up to make rags. If you don't have enough space in your closet, consider storing extra sheet sets under a bed in a container on wheels.

For your guest bedroom, keep a pair of sheets and a set of towels in an under-

Vacuum-Seal Bags

I am often asked about the vacuum-seal bags that are on the market. They are the bags that you use with your vacuum to suck out all the air so more things can be stored in smaller spaces. The bags are pretty pricey.

I have asked many women who have used them if they have worked for them and less than a handful said they liked them. The bags may be useful for bulky items that have a lot of air in them—pillows and comforters—but the bags don't stack well, and they are heavy when they are stuffed full. Full bags also have a greater chance of leaking. They are hard to reuse because they won't stay sealed. They seem to work at first but often leak, which is why I personally do not recommend them.

the-bed container. It saves space, and the added bonus is you will always have clean towels and sheets when guests come. Also tuck in a few convenience items in this container that you can put out in a basket for guests to make them feel welcome: bath gel, lotion, a toothbrush, and toothpaste.

To store sheets, sort them into sets for each bed size. To save space and to keep them folded neatly together, place them inside the matching pillowcase. Seasonal sheets can be stored with other seasonal linens, stacked behind your everyday sheets or stored on the top shelf. Label the shelves with the size of the sheets. Or, using a fine-tipped permanent marking pen, you can write the size on the bottom of the sheets for easy identification.

The top shelf can be dedicated to infrequently used items, such as pillows, quilts, or seasonal towels and sheets. You may want to cover these with an old sheet to help keep dust off of them.

Place table linens on another shelf; a basket can hold napkins if needed. Label this shelf also. If there is limited room in the closet, or for convenience, store linens in the rooms where they are used (i.e., table linens in a dining room sideboard, sheets in the bedrooms).

For the sundry items stored here, separate by type and store them in appropriate-sized containers. Label them to help family members know where to find things and where to put them back.

If you are storing medicines in this closet, keep them secure from children. Be sure to check expiration dates and take those that have expired to your pharmacist for proper disposal. Expired medicine is considered hazardous waste; it stands to reason it should be disposed of as such. If your pharmacist won't take it, call other pharmacies or contact your local hazardous waste facility to see what disposal method they recommend. It is no longer considered safe to throw expired medicine down the toilet or to put it in the trash. Do not leave the Green Light as you sort medications. Put expired medicines in the BE basket; if there are little children keep it away from them.

I recommend separating first aid supplies from medicines. Keep them handy in a basket or plastic container with a lid. Separate items by placing them in sandwich bags or small containers.

WRAP UP

You will love getting linens out of your closet without having to search. Give yourself a cheer and a pat on the back. You deserve a reward. You did it! Wasn't that easy and fun? And doesn't it feel good?

Your linen closet will stay organized because:

- Frequently used items are kept in convenient places. Seldom-used items are kept on higher or lower shelves.

- The towels, sheets, and table linens are neatly folded and stacked separately.
- Family members can fold towels and sheets and put them where they belong.
- Labeled containers hold extra personal items stored here.
- Only current medicines are kept here, and they are contained and secure.
- Labeling has made it easy for things to be put away where they belong.
- Everything has a designated place, and everything will be in its place.

Congratulations on a job well done!

The Bathroom

(9)

After the entryway or living room, the bathroom is the second most important room to keep clean and organized. Bathrooms are busy little rooms where we keep a lot of useful things. Family members use the room often during the day, and guests will most likely see this room during their visit. It's the room where most of us start our days.

The bathroom can also be a sanctuary—the one place you can lock the door, turn up some music, and be alone. You can relax in a warm bath and read, or cry without anyone hearing you. (And as a parent, if you turn the music up loud enough, you can't hear the kids fighting.) An organized bathroom will add to the peace and serenity you can find in this personal space.

SEARCHLIGHT

Take a good look around the bathroom and look for what you like about the room and what you don't like. Write it in your notebook. What is the wattage you feel when you are in this room (see page 15)? Is this a room where you can relax and enjoy a warm shower or soak in a bubble bath? It won't be relaxing if your wattage is under a 7.

1. What do you like about this room?
2. What don't you like in this room? Identify needs by asking yourself the following questions:
   a. Are things organized so they are convenient to use?
   b. Is the countertop a clutter magnet?
   c. Is there a place to hang towels?
   d. Are tub toys out of the tub between bath times?
   e. Is makeup contained? Are the cosmetics out-dated?
   f. Do you need more room for storage?
   g. Are medications stored in this room? Is this the best and safest place to keep them?

If your bathroom is very tiny, it may seem impossible to find room for all the things that belong there, especially if there is no storage space in the room. But large bathrooms can also have storage issues. If every shelf and drawer is overflowing, it's much harder to find what you need. Take photos of the room and the interior of the cupboards in it.

Now that you have looked at this room and decided what you like and don't like about it, you can move on to using the Spotlight to set goals to improve the bathroom.

> "My kids always perceived the bathroom as a place where you wait it out until all the groceries are unloaded from the car."
>
> —ERMA BOMBECK

Paula's Story

Do you ever have mornings like Paula? As she was rushing to get ready for the day, she realized she had run out of toothpaste and had forgotten to put it on her grocery list. Someone had borrowed her hair dryer and hadn't put it back, so she had to spend precious moments trying to find it. She spent several minutes searching for a specific lipstick color she wanted to wear because she couldn't find the tube. Her eyeliner was dried out, and she tossed it back into the assortment of used up and usable makeup. The trash can wasn't convenient, so she simply tossed used tissues on the counter. She felt frustrated and harried before even leaving the house.

SPOTLIGHT

Now that you have written down the problems you saw in this room, write down the goals you want to accomplish. As you complete each one, check it off. Here are some examples of goals you could set for this room:

1. Solve storage problems by using every available space in the room. You can hang a shoe organizer on the back of the door for small items, place items under the sink, install shelves or free-standing racks above the toilet, and place a plastic cart with drawers on the floor if there is space.

2. Keep the countertop free of clutter.

3. Install hooks or use a free-standing hat rack to hang towels.

4. Use containers for cosmetics, towels, and toiletries.

5. Assign places to store everything where it will be easy for all family members to return items after use.

6. Guests will be able to use this room without you needing to do anything except get them a clean hand towel—no apologizes needed.

If you need to purchase any containers or shelves, measure the space in the drawers, under the sink, and in any other cupboard and decide what you will be using the containers for before setting off to buy them.

GREEN LIGHT

With your goals determined and written down and with your mind focused on what you want this room to be like, it is time to use the Green Light to take action. There are a few ideal times to work on this room: either before anyone else is up in the morning, after everyone has left for the day, or while the children are napping. Set your timer for one hour and see how much you can get done. If you need to work in smaller amounts of time, that is fine. If, after one hour, you need more time, either set your timer again and keep on organizing or reach a good stopping point and schedule a date in the future to finish organizing the room. Soon it will look just how you want it to.

As always, start working from the inside out. As you take things out of the cupboards and drawers, things will look chaotic, but they will look and function better when you are finished.

I suggest you work in this order:

1. drawers
2. cupboards
3. under the sink
4. medicine cabinet
5. other shelves and storage spaces
6. countertop
7. shower and bathtub

Gather your tool kit (see page 22) and your four containers (see page 35). Wear comfy clothes and keep a snack and drink handy.

Drawers

Take everything out one drawer at a time. Wipe out each drawer with a damp cloth. Start with the top drawer and work your way down to the bottom one.

In one drawer (or more than one drawer if they are small and you have the space), put your cosmetics, dividing them between containers for makeup and skin care products. Use containers to keep things from sliding around and becoming a jumbled mess. This will also give you more space. To keep the containers in place, attach them in the drawers with wide, double-stick tape.

As you put your cosmetics into the containers inside each drawer, limit the number of products you keep. Donate those unused samples you think you will use "someday" but never have. Or write a goal to use them within the week and if you don't, then donate them and you can check off another goal. Keep only the cosmetics you use on a regular basis in the premium spaces (see page 24). Cotton balls, cotton swabs, etc., can be placed in their own decorative containers and kept on the countertop, in a drawer, or in a cupboard.

As you place your makeup in containers, make sure the makeup is usable and you actually wear it. Some guidelines for the shelf life of makeup are: First, if it smells or has a distinct unusual odor, throw it away! Second, if you can't remember when you purchased it, throw it away. Natural cosmetics do not last as long as those with extra preservatives in them. You want to replace your makeup because of germs and bacteria. Most likely, you'll get bored with your makeup before it expires, so a good rule to follow is to toss the color if you stop wearing it for a few months.

If you keep hair ribbons, elastics, barrettes, and other hair accessories in the bathroom, contain likes together in different containers. If the ribbons get tangled together consider hanging them from a swing-out hanger or on mug hooks attached to the wall.

Perfumes, lotions, deodorant, hair brushes, and combs all need to have their own containers. Curling irons/flat irons, and hair dryers either need to be hung on a hook or placed in a drawer. Be sure to wind up the cords to save space and prevent tangles (it also looks nicer).

Toothpaste, dental floss, and mouthwash can be stored together in the same area. If you never use the sample-size oral care items you receive from your dentist's office, don't accept the samples at your future visits. However, these sample sizes are nice for travel. If you use them for travel, don't put them in your premium space, put them with your travel items, which should be kept in a different cupboard or shelf, or in your luggage.

Tip: If you share a drawer with someone, the only way to successfully do this is to have separate containers for each person.

Men also need containers for deodorants, brushes, combs, shaving creams, gels, lotions, after-shave, razors, toothbrushes, toothpaste, and dental floss.

Cupboards

Take everything out of the cupboards one shelf at a time and wipe off each shelf. Organize the shelves the same way you do the drawers. Place like items together on the shelves, such as extra shampoo, personal items, bubble bath, soaps, tissues, or hair accessories. If the items are small, keep them together by placing them in containers.

Towels that are stored in cupboards can be stacked by type. Label the shelf with the size of towel that goes in that spot (bath towel, hand towel, or washcloth). See Chapter 8 for more information on storing bath linens.

Under the Sink

Start by clearing everything out from under the sink. Wipe this area clean with a damp cloth. This area is great for storing bottles of shampoo, conditioner, hand cleaner, toilet paper, and assorted personal items. This space is a semi-storage area as you don't use the items here every day, but you want to keep them in the bathroom. If your bathroom is very small, under the sink could be considered a premium space if you use it daily. You may have baskets that hold items you pull out and use every day. Keep like items together in containers. These can be easily removed to reach what you need.

Bins that can be pulled out make it easy to see what is under the sink. Some bins have runners on the bottom that attach with screws to the bottom of the shelf. Or you can have pull-out bins built in. Plastic containers are the best choice for under the sink in case the pipes leak.

If you don't have a cupboard under the sink, a narrow container with or without wheels with pull-out drawers is an option. If you don't want to see what is in the drawers, use containers that are opaque or that are your favorite color.

To make more space under the sink, add wire shelves. They come in stainless steel or covered with white plastic. They can be placed on just one side of the cupboard so taller items can be stored on the other side.

I recommend keeping a little caddy of cleaning supplies under the sink as it is convenient and saves time to have this in every bathroom. Install child locks on the doors if there are children in the home or if you have young children who sometimes use the bathrooms.

Medicine Cabinet

Separate medicines from first-aid supplies and vitamins. A bin, basket, or other adequate container works well to store medicines in. To begin, round up all medicines from every place in the home (bathrooms, kitchen, closets, bedrooms).

> **Tip:** *The bathroom is not the best place to store medicines. They should be stored in a cool, dry place. High humidity can actually affect the potency of certain drugs. Store medicines on a shelf in the linen closet, hall closet, or some other*

closet. If there are children in the home, take safety precautions to keep them from having access to the medicines. Medications frequently used can be kept on a shelf in the kitchen where they are convenient to take.

Separate medicines into like categories: pain relief, antiseptics, cold and flu, fever reducer, ointments, antacids, and all other over-the-counter medicines you have.

You can have a large container to hold all medicine and then place smaller containers in it to keep like meds together. Or small containers can be labeled and kept next to the larger container. Vitamins can be in a smaller container within the larger one or next to it. First-aid supplies can also be in a bin and kept near the medicine bin.

For prescription medicines, place bottles in separate resealable bags with the person's name and Rx printed on the outside. This is especially helpful in the middle of the night when looking for a specific medicine for a family member.

Always check the expiration dates. Medicines can become toxic or lose their effectiveness past the expiration date. Check expiration dates twice a year. A good time to remember to do this is when changing to and from daylight savings time. (This is also a good time to check the batteries in your smoke detectors.)

Clear everything out of the medicine cabinet and wipe it clean with a damp cloth. Put items here that are used every day that either don't fit in a drawer or aren't handy to get to, if in a drawer. Toothbrushes, toothpaste, deodorant, after-shave, perfume, hairspray, face wash, etc., are examples of things to put in a "medicine cabinet."

If you keep first-aid supplies in your bathroom, I recommend the ointments, sprays, and adhesive bandages be kept in a container with a lid. Keep this container in a drawer in the room. Children may climb to get to the bandages kept in the cabinet and fall and hurt themselves. If you do have children, for safety sake install child locks on cupboards and drawers.

Other Shelves and Storage Spaces

A small set of shelves or a small cupboard are great for storing towels, lotions, toilet paper, facial tissue, or other items you want to keep convenient to use.

If you have a very small bathroom, you can use an over-the-door shoe organizer to hold a variety of items such as toothpaste, face wash, nail products, hair dryer, curling iron, makeup (kept in zipper bags), after-shave, extra soaps (kept in a container), razors, cotton balls (in a bag), and just about anything else that would traditionally be stored in a drawer.

Other storage places for hand towels or washcloths could be in a basket on the back of the toilet. Free-standing shelves designed to fit over the toilet can hold larger towels, toilet paper, and other toiletries.

Countertop

The best way to keep the countertop from being cluttered is to have a specific storage place for everything in the bathroom. Label drawers if you need to help family members learn where things belong. Now that your drawers are organized, it should be easy to put away all of the items you've been leaving on the counter.

Only allow a select few items on the counter—things such as electric toothbrushes, soap in a dispenser (to keep the sink area cleaner), electric razor charger (or it can go in a drawer and be taken out when needed), a holder for toothbrushes and toothpaste, a candle or other attractive items limited to one to three depending on the size of the countertop.

Reading material in the bathroom can be placed in a basket and kept on the counter if there is space, or it can be kept on the floor near where it is read (by the tub or toilet). The same rule applies to this reading material as in the other rooms. Get rid of old issues of magazines and catalogs. Do not let them take root and live here. Rotate them in and out, discarding old issues at least every three months.

If your countertop is long and you have plenty of space, place a tray on it to hold perfumes, hair spray, hair gel, and other personal items you use often.

Tip: Decorative soaps are pretty, but if they aren't used, they become dust collectors and your decoration will quickly become an eyesore.

Shower and Bathtub

Placing things like shampoos, razors, and bubble bath on the rim of the bathtub gives the room a cluttered look. If it is a large tub with jets, there will be room to hold a few items on the rim, but contain them in an attractive basket or on a flat, small tray.

If your tub is also the shower area, an over-the-shower organizer holds soap, shampoos, conditioners, and washcloths. Another option is a pole organizer that has a spring rod and fits in the corner of the tub. This kind of organizer comes in several different styles and is made out of plastic or stainless steel. These can hold everything you need in the tub or shower so you don't have to use the tub rim for any products.

In a child's bathroom, install sturdy hooks for each child to hang his or her bath towel on after it is used. Give each child a different colored towel, and it will be easy to see who needs a reminder to use his or her hook. Label the hooks with the children's names.

If there is not room for hooks, or you need more space than just one towel rod provides, a free-standing coat rack spray painted to match the bathroom is an option. Or attach a towel rack to the wall.

To keep tub toys out of the tub between baths, place them in a mesh bag that hangs from the faucet or from suction cups on the shower wall. They can also be placed in a plastic container and put under the sink. Check the toys regularly for mold and mildew.

Tip: *Do not save slivers of soap. They just create a mess in your shower or tub. Toss the old sliver as soon as you open a new bar of soap.*

WRAP UP

I am proud of you! Your bathroom will stay organized because you have:
- Placed everything in containers when you possibly could.
- Utilized all the space in your bathroom (back of the door, shelves, hooks), finding room for everything that needs to be in here.
- Assigned places for everything.
- Donated or gotten rid of items you never use, cosmetics, samples you were given, etc.
- Installed hooks, or other towel racks, so there is a place for towels to be hung up after being used.
- Installed safety locks to keep children safe.
- Moved first-aid supplies and medicines out of the medicine cabinet.
- Created a clutter-free counter by having containers for the things kept there.
- Contained tub toys and removed them from the tub.

Now tell yourself you did a good job and be proud of all you accomplished!

The Family Room

The family room is an informal, comfortable room where family members gather and entertain friends in a less formal area than the living room. It is an all-purpose room used for relaxing, talking, reading, watching television, and doing other family activities.

Getting this room to work for you is very important as so many activities are done here. Because it's used so often for so many things, this room seems to collect stuff. Keeping the clutter under control will help you get the most out of this area. Not everything has to be out of sight to be free of clutter. Things just need to have a home and be contained and easily accessible for all family members.

SEARCHLIGHT

To organize this room, start with your Searchlight and look for things you like about this room. Does this room light you up when you are in it? Do you feel comfortable, relaxed, and happy? Is this a place you want to be in with your family? Take a picture so you can do a before-and-after comparison. Then ask yourself these questions and record your answers in a notebook:

Arrange your family room so it can comfortably accommodate all of your family activities.

1. What do you like about this room?
2. What don't you like about this room? Identify needs by asking the following questions:
   a. What does your family use this room for (watching television, playing games, reading, eating meals, doing homework, folding clothes, and doing craft projects)?
   b. Is the room comfortably arranged for family members to do various activities?
   c. Are the flat surfaces, such as the entertainment center, end tables, and coffee table, free of clutter?
   d. Are there assigned places for everything that needs to be in this room (games, remote controls, magazines, books, lap quilts, DVDs, toys, etc.)?
   e. Are things "dumped" in this room because no one knows where else to put them? Is it home to things like school papers, newspapers, magazines, and old toys?
   f. Are there things that you can get rid of?
   g. How did the family room get in this shape? What steps can be taken to improve it?

Paula's Story

Here's what Paula found in her family room when she used her Searchlight. There were dirty dishes shoved under the end tables and left out on the coffee table. Magazines were left on the couch and newspapers were scattered on the floor.

The lap quilts she and her family liked to snuggle under to watch television were left in a heaped pile on the floor. Glue and papers were left out from a project her son was working on. There was a game closet, but the games were always falling out, and she found many loose puzzle pieces from different puzzles.

Empty DVD cases were strewn about the room, and next to the couch, the ironing board was set up with the iron cord plugged in, just waiting for an accident to happen as it was in a high-traffic area of the room. She was discouraged with what she saw.

Paula did like that it was a gathering place for the children after school and that it was close to the kitchen. She liked many of the things that were in the room but not the disorganization she found.

3. Now you have taken a good look at this room and what's in it, how does it make you feel? Are you lit up on the wattage scale at a 7 or above (see page 15)?

After you answer these questions in your notebook, you can move on to the Spotlight to set goals and make changes.

SPOTLIGHT

With the Searchlight, you did a good job finding things that work and don't work in this room. Now you can use the Spotlight to set goals that will make you happy and will create a family room where everyone likes to be and feels comfortable.

You wrote down the things you didn't like; now write down your goals. As you accomplish each one, you can check it off. Here are some examples of goals you could set for this room:

1. It will be inviting and comfortable for everyone in the family.
2. Furniture will be arranged so everyone can enjoy doing activities here.
3. The game closet will be organized so games are easily accessible. Each game will be checked for missing pieces. Incomplete games will be tossed.
4. DVDs will be kept in their cases (or in a large DVD holder) and will be stored in the entertainment center.
5. Magazine racks or baskets will be placed by chairs so magazines and newspapers are convenient to put away.
6. Books will be organized on the bookshelf.
7. Rules will be established about eating in the room.
8. There will be a place for craft projects to be created with storage available for the projects when they are not being worked on.
9. Place a container at the end of the couch or nearby to hold lap quilts.
10. Children's toys will be placed in a container. Unused toys will be donated. A limited amount of toys will be allowed in the family room if children's toys are stored in their bedrooms. If their toys are mainly kept in the family room, containers will be used for toys. Refer to Chapter 7 for further information on toys.
11. Every item that does not have a wattage of 7 or above will be replaced. This can be done over a period of time.

12. A family meeting will be held to discuss what can and cannot be kept in this room (e.g., no shoes, dirty dishes, unfinished craft projects, etc.).
13. Everything in the room will have its own designated space, including the remote controls for all electronic systems.

If you need to buy any containers, take measurements for the areas where they will be used and set a time to buy them. Set a deadline for getting the room organized and move into the Green Light to go organize.

GREEN LIGHT

With your goals written down, you now have the Green Light to move forward. Go as slow or as fast as you want, but I recommend you schedule a specific time to work in this room. Try setting your timer for an hour and play beat the clock. See how much you can get accomplished in that hour. Then reset the timer and keep on going until you are done. Or schedule another time to come back—it could be in the evening or the next day. Stay in the Green Light for the entire hour by not leaving the room. Take the phone off the hook or let the answering machine earn its keep, and return calls after you are done. Wear comfortable clothes. Have your tool kit with you (see page 22) and grab your four containers (see page 35). Get yourself a snack and a drink and get started. You are all set to turn up the wattage in this room! Remember, it will look worse as you are working in this room, but it will all come together and everything will look great when you are finished. When you need to take a break, I recommend setting the timer for five minutes to remind you to come back.

As always, start working from the inside out. I suggest you work in this order (completely organize one area of the room before you move on to the next area):

1. entertainment center
2. bookcases
3. closet
4. toy boxes

5. flat surfaces, such as:
   a. tables
   b. fireplace mantel and hearth
   c. game tables—Ping-Pong, foosball, table hockey, pool, etc.

Entertainment Center

Take everything out of the entertainment center one section at a time. If there are shelves, start there. Dust off the shelf and only put back the things that belong there. This could include instruction manuals, CDs, DVDs, Blu-ray discs, videos, or electronic games. Group like things together, so all DVDs go on one shelf, manuals go on another, etc. Put the things that don't belong in the entertainment center elsewhere in the room if they belong in the room or put them in one of the four containers (trash, recycle, donate, or BE basket) if they don't belong in the room.

After completing every shelf, move on to the drawers. Take everything out of the drawers one at a time, starting with the top drawer. Before you place things back in the drawers, decide what will go in each drawer and remember to keep

Organizing DVDs

There are countless ways to organize your DVDs. The most important thing is to find a system that you can and will follow. If you're not a highly structured person, don't try to maintain a highly structured system. Personally, I think just having all of the DVDs in one place works well. Decide where to keep them and then keep them there; that's all you need to do. If you're looking for more structure than that, you can:

> It's most important to find a system you can and will follow.

1. Place them in a DVD stand that has slots that hold them in place.
2. Organize the discs by subject: drama, comedy, family, action. If you do this and you want the cases to stay separated by subject, apply a different colored dot for each subject (e.g., drama—red, comedy—green, etc.).
3. If you have a large DVD collection and want to save space, remove the discs from their cases and place the discs in a binder specifically made for DVD storage. If you are organizing by subject, you could have a case for each subject. These cases will fit nicely on a shelf in your entertainment center or on a bookshelf.
4. Consider renting or checking out DVDs from the library to save money and space.

Whatever method you use, make it as easy as possible to put the discs away after they are used. All of these organizing ideas will work for CDs, Blu-ray, and video games as well.

Control the Dirty Dishes

Are you constantly finding dirty dishes in the family room? Consider establishing a rule that all family members must take their dishes to the kitchen as soon as they leave the family room. If someone doesn't follow the rule and you are the person who removes the dishes, charge the person maid wages for your services. As the family member pays for maid service, his or her skills in taking dishes out of the room will improve. If the family member doesn't have money of his or her own, he or she can work it off by doing a chore of your choice (like washing dishes or loading and unloading the dishwasher). Make up a list of chores family members can choose from and post it inside a cupboard door.

like things together. If you find DVDs or other items in the drawer that belong on the shelf, move those items to the proper shelf. If you keep like things together, when you are looking for an item, you'll only need to look in one place.

If your family has video-game systems, place a lidless container in the entertainment center to hold all of the cords and remote controls. This way, all the cords and controls are in one place and they are easy to get out and easy to put away. You can have another container for the games, or follow one of the methods suggested in the organizing DVDs sidebar (on page 151).

Check every DVD, CD, Blu-ray, and video game case kept in the entertainment center to make sure the disc is in it. If the disc is missing, keep the case out and ask family members to search for the missing disc later. Don't get distracted and start searching for it now. Stay focused on your overall organizing plan for the room.

Bookcases

Remove all the books one shelf at a time and dust the shelf and books. As you remove the books put them in categories (children, young adult, geography, science, etc.). As you place them back on the shelves, put them together by category. I recommend removing the dust covers because they get tattered and the dust settles on the top of the book, not the front and back sides.

You can place tattered or awkward-sized paperback books in a photo-holder box that is labeled with the titles of the books.

You can also use the bookshelf to hold boxes of craft items if you or your family members work on crafts in this room. Make sure the craft items are conveniently and attractively contained.

Closet

If you have a closet in this room, decide what you want to use it for: Games and crafts are good options. Limit what you keep here so you can get maximum use out of this premium space (see page 24). Clear everything out of the closet. Decide if each item belongs in this closet or if it would be better in another closet. Don't leave the room, just put things that don't belong here in the BE basket and deal with them later. Dust all of the empty shelves. Then group the items that belong in the closet together by category and give each category its own shelf or part of a shelf. Check each item before you put it back in the closet to make sure your family still enjoys and uses the item and the item is still in good enough shape to use.

Let Your Décor Light You Up

Evaluate the amount of decorations you have in your family room, specifically on the hearth and mantel. How do they make you feel? Is your wattage a 7 or above when you look at them? If there are too many things in this room that make it look cluttered, consider rotating decorations in and out or rearranging them to avoid a cluttered feeling in the room. Evaluate each knickknack and decide if you can give it away so someone else can enjoy it. Be honest when you are evaluating each item. Get rid of anything that no longer lights you up. You could also take a picture of knickknacks before donating them and put the photo in an album to bring back memories.

You'll likely have games here, so check each game to make sure it is complete with no missing pieces that prevent playing the game. If a game isn't complete and it can't or won't be played because of the missing piece, get rid of it. If your family has outgrown the game or never plays it, put it in your donation box. Store like games together (card games, board games, children's games, etc.). If the boxes are falling apart, tape them back together before placing them back on the shelf. For small games, plastic containers or metal boxes that are labeled are good, sturdy containers to use. For larger games, purchase plastic Game Savers boxes. Game Savers boxes are sturdy, plastic containers to organize and store your games. The lid is attached, and there are compartments for the different game pieces. They are available online, including on my Web site, www.marilynbohn.com.

Toy Boxes

Keep toys confined to one place. Toys don't have to be kept in boxes. A plastic cart with stackable drawers or bins lets you separate toys by category (dolls, trucks, etc.). A toy box without a lid makes it easier for children to get out and put away their toys. The size of the container limits the amount of toys in the room. It may be more practical for you to have a few different, smaller containers when your child is very young so the child can easily reach into the containers. See Chapter 7 for more ideas on organizing toys.

Flat Surfaces

Tables: Clear everything off the end tables and dust them. Then decide what belongs on them. End tables are good for holding a lamp, a few family photos, or souvenirs from family trips (limit the number to three or under depending on the size of the table). Sort the items you're not placing back on the table into one of your four containers (trash, recycle, donate, or BE basket) or find a home for the item somewhere else in the room. Remember to keep likes together; if it's a DVD or book, place it with others like it. On the coffee table, three to five magazines neatly stacked or a few books and a centerpiece leave enough room for bowls of snacks and drinking glasses. Make coasters available and teach your family members to use them. The coasters will help prevent water marks on the furniture.

> **Tip:** *To keep track of remote controls, designate a basket for them. Keep the basket on the table where they are used most often, near a chair or on the coffee table. If young children play with the remotes, place the basket out of their reach. The more convenient they are to get to, the easier they will be to put back in the basket. If there are remotes that are used infrequently, place those in a separate basket and keep them in the entertainment center. Only keep those out that are used frequently.*

Laundry in the Family Room

Do you like to watch television while you iron and fold laundry? There's nothing wrong with that, but to keep the family room organized, put the laundry in baskets to be delivered to the bedrooms as soon as you finish folding them. When you are finished ironing, immediately unplug the iron and wind up the cord to prevent any accidents. Let the iron cool and then put it and the ironing board away. Make space for the board in a closet or in the laundry room. Leaving the board out takes up valuable space and makes it hard to relax because you're constantly reminded of that chore. If you clean up your projects, you set a good example for your family members, and they will be more likely to honor the rules you establish for keeping the room clean and organized.

Fireplace Mantel: Take everything off the mantel and dust it. To keep the family room from having a cluttered look, do not over crowd this area by having too many things placed here. Possible things to put back on the mantel are figurines, candles, holiday decorations, collections, or family photos.

Fireplace Hearth: Remove everything and dust the hearth, or wash it well. You can keep your hearth clear with nothing on it at all, or keep floor pillows and quilts stacked in a basket there. If you build fires in your fireplace, you can keep a container of wood and the fireplace tool on the hearth.

Game Tables: Surfaces such as Ping-Pong, foosball, air hockey, and pool tables can be clutter magnets. When someone wants to play, they either have to unload the table or not use it at all. At a family meeting, enlist everyone's help in agreeing that these will not be used as dumping grounds. If everything in the room has a designated place other than that table, it will be easier to keep it clutter-free.

WRAP UP

Now that you have organized your family room, it is a comfortable place used by all members of the family. Doesn't it feel good to have a home for everything and to have everything arranged in a pleasant and inviting manner?

You really did a good job working on your goals and completing all of them. It can be a lot of work to get things just as you want them, and you did it! Don't you feel good about what you just accomplished? Give yourself a pat on the back!

Congratulations on:

- setting your goals and checking each one off as you finished
- getting the DVDs, video games, CDs, and Blu-ray discs organized in the entertainment center
- organizing the books in the bookcase; donating those no longer being read; mending books you keep; and removing the covers to make the books look tidy on the shelves
- placing containers in convenient locations for crafts, newspapers, magazines, and quilts
- holding a family meeting to establish rules about eating in the family room and what is expected
- sorting through the games and keeping the ones that are used
- containing the toys in an easy-to-use way
- assigning places for everything

Because of all the things you did, it will be easier for your family to keep this room organized. Now use the wattage scale to rate how you feel in this room.

(11) Home Office and Paperwork

When you think of paper in your home, do you cringe from the sheer volume that you have to deal with every day? How long has it been since you saw the top of your desk? Are papers scattered all over your house? Do you have a working filing system? Do you blame yourself for the paper clutter in your home? It is not your fault paper has become such a large organizing problem. We receive more mail and paperwork in one day than our grandparents received in a month. The good news is that a good, working filing system can help you virtually eliminate the paper piles in your home.

You need an effective plan for dealing with the papers that manage to find their way into your home. This chapter will help you take control of your incoming mail and get your files and home office organized.

SEARCHLIGHT

With the Searchlight, look in each room in your home where you have paper stashed—in the kitchen, office, family room, living room, the bedroom(s), and anywhere else paper may be piled. In your notebook, answer these questions:

1. What currently works in your paperwork system? Write down whatever you do that helps you answer the mail, pay bills, and complete other deadlines on time.

2. Is paper a hassle for you, and is it taking over your life? Identify what you need to change by asking yourself the following questions:

    a. Is mail sorted and dealt with in a timely manner?

    b. Is there a landing place for all papers that come into your home? Is there a place for mail?

    c. Do you have a hard time deciding what to keep and what to toss?

    d. Does junk mail live in your home?

    e. Is the desk area functional? Do you use this area, or do you answer mail and pay bills in another area? Are all the items that you use to pay bills and to respond to other correspondence organized and within easy reach (calculator, calendar, pens, postage, envelopes, etc.)?

    f. What is the condition of the filing system? Is the current one working for you and is it efficient?

    g. Do you need to reduce the personal items and decorations on your desk to create more work space?

    h. Do you have adequate lighting?

    i. Is there space to store office supplies, such as paper and other necessities?

    j. Are there items you need to relocate, donate, recycle, or trash to reduce clutter in your office?

Paula's Story

Paula was dismayed when it came to the volume of paper she had to deal with every day. She brings in the mail as soon as she arrives home from work. She tears open the envelopes, glances at the contents, and then tosses the papers wherever she happens to be at the moment.

She doesn't have time to really look through the mail, and it stresses her out to make decisions on what to do with it, so she ignores it day after day. She has a filing cabinet, but it is chock-full of old papers that she filed years ago. She is not sure what is in there now. She would like a good filing system but doesn't know how to set it up. She also wants to be in control of all the mail she receives.

k. Is your desk or work area organized to support the activities you do here? Does this place help you to be creative and accomplish tasks efficiently?

l. What activities do you do at your desk or work station? What supplies do you need?

m. Is the layout and flow comfortable and efficient?

n. What will help you enjoy working here?

Use the wattage scale (see page 15) to assess how you feel. Are you lit up at a 7 or above? Now that you have answered these questions and written the things down that you want to change, use the Spotlight to set goals to increase the wattage of your home office and deal with your paper. Take a photo of your home office area for a before-and-after comparison.

It may have been painful to find out just how much paper has piled up and made you feel out of control, but now that you know what the problems are, you can use the Spotlight and set goals. You will no longer dread the mail, and your filing system will work smoothly for you.

You wrote down what problems you see; now write down your goals. They can be checked off as you accomplish them. Here are some examples of goals you could set to conquer the paperwork nightmare:

1. Establish a landing place for all mail and put the mail only in this place and nowhere else.
2. Have all supplies needed to pay bills, answer letters, and take care of all correspondence (letter opener, scissors, envelopes, cards, stamps, pens, and rubber bands) in a portable container or in desk drawers.
3. Schedule a time when you can open your mail and sort it every day.
4. Set up an efficient, easy-to-use filing system.
5. Remove your name from mailing lists to reduce the amount of junk mail you receive (see page 164).
6. Create space for office supplies, such as computer paper, paper clips, stapler, hole punch, tape, sticky notes, and extra pens and pencils.

If you don't have file drawers, a file box, or file cabinets, purchase one. I recommend a 22" (56cm) or 26" (66cm), two-drawer or four-drawer cabinet and check to be sure the drawers pull out all the way. In my experience, the 18" (46cm), two-drawer file cabinets do not give you enough room and the drawers don't pull out all the way.

The size of the file cabinet you need depends on how much information you want to store in the files. If the cabinet is small, you can place a printer on it or it can possibly be treated as furniture and used as an end table by placing an attractive cover, such as a small tablecloth, table runner or placemat on it. Larger file cabinets require a place of their own.

If you don't have room for or don't want to purchase a file cabinet, the next best option is a file box. Cardboard or plastic banker boxes with lids are sold at office-supply and variety stores. I recommend the plastic ones as they last longer and are more attractive and can protect against water damage. These can be placed next to your work area or under a table or stored in the closet on the shelf or on the floor.

You'll also need a shredder so you can dispose of personal information in a secure way.

GREEN LIGHT

With your goals written down, start working in the Green Light. Paperwork is a huge task to conquer, so we're going to break it down into easy sections. I suggest you work in this order:

1. mail
2. loose papers
3. filing
4. home office area

Mail

We're starting with mail because implementing a plan right away will keep the paper mess from growing. Deal with the new before you deal with the old. This is an approach you need to commit to each day to keep your paperwork and mail organized. Decide on a landing place for your mail when you bring it into your home. Designate a basket specifically for the mail and place the mail in its designated spot as soon as you bring it in the house. If it is tossed on the desk or on the kitchen counter or on a table in the family entryway and it is not contained, it can become scattered, and it will become out-of-control clutter. Leave the mail until you have time to sit down and look at it carefully enough to make a decision about everything, but toss all obvious junk mail immediately.

How to Stop Receiving Junk Mail

Take control of your paper by *reducing* the amount of paper coming into your home. One of the most effective ways to reduce the amount of paper you receive is to get your name and address removed from mailing lists. Here are some web sites where you can remove yourself from junk mail lists:

www.proquo.com

www.obviously.com/junkmail

www.41pounds.org

www.optoutprescreen.com

You can choose what mail you want to receive and what you don't. You can get your name removed from coupon lists, catalogs, and insurance and credit card lists to name a few.

Keep a trash can or recycling bin next to your landing zone so this is easy. When opening mail, have your office supplies and your calendar or planner handy to jot down information you need later. This is absolutely essential!

When you sit down to sort your mail, make a goal to handle each piece of paper only once. Make a decision while the piece of mail is in your hand, without putting it down into a pile. If you want to get rid of paper piles in your life, you need to make decisions as you sort through paper. As you look at each piece of paper, ask "what action do I need to take?" Use this 4-D plan of action:

1. *Done:* This is something that doesn't need your immediate attention and you can recycle, shred, toss, or file it for reference (junk mail, a magazine that goes to your reading basket, tax information, etc.).

2. *Do:* If it is something that takes less than two minutes to do, do it right then (clip a coupon and put in your coupon holder or planner, RSVP for an event, etc.).
3. *Delegate:* Pass it off to the person who is to take care of it.
4. *Delivery* (short-term and long-term): Short-term delivery is something that needs action within a few days. Make a note in your planner or on your calendar and put it in a basket or an action file folder to be taken care of in a few days (a bill to pay, correspondence, etc.). If it hasn't been done in a few days, re-evaluate when action needs to be taken, write the new date in your planner as a reminder, and file it away in your filing cabinet where it can stay until you are ready to take care of it. Long-term delivery is for filing resource information, projects you are working on, or files to be kept permanently (insurance papers, travel information, warranties, and other information you want to keep for a long period of time but don't refer to very often).

You can tweak the 4-D plan to meet your needs. When you make a decision and take action as you sort the mail, you will no longer create piles of papers. If you have piles now, start with the most recent and sort using the 4-D plan. Here are some examples:

Let's pretend you just received an invitation to a wedding shower. You decide you want to go to this so you write it on your calendar or in your planner. If you need to RSVP, do it now by e-mail or phone. This was a Do action because it took less than two minutes. Then file the invitation for reference in the folder that corresponds with the date of the shower. Or if you don't need to keep the invitation, recycle it.

Another example: Pretend an advertisement for lawn care is in the mail. Your husband wanted help with the yard so you put it in a place for him to review. This was a Delegate action.

Let's say you get an advertisement for bathtub refinishing. Does your bathtub need refinishing? If this is something you are interested in, put it in the folder labeled coupons/offers. Or, if you are not interested in this service, place it in the recycle bin. This is a Done action because you didn't have to actually do anything with it right then other than to put it in the recycle bin or a folder. If you decide to use it later, you can find it.

To save you even more time sorting the mail, request your utility companies and credit card companies send you electronic bills instead of paper bills. And going one step further, pay your bills online either to the companies directly or set up bill payment through your financial institution. I suggest setting up one e-mail address for all the electronic confirmation e-mails that come from all the different companies.

We will talk about how long to keep paper bills later in the filing section.

Now that you have tackled your mail, you can move on to the loose papers around the house.

Loose Papers

Step into the Green Light by gathering all the loose papers around your home into one container. If you fill that container, get another one and keep gathering. Set your timer for thirty minutes to complete this goal.

At the end of thirty minutes, you can start the next phase if you are feeling "lit up" and have energy. If you are feeling overwhelmed, set your timer for five minutes, walk away, get a drink, take some deep breaths, and come back when the five minutes are up so you can start the next step.

Set your timer for another thirty minutes and start sorting through the papers. Look at each piece of paper and ask yourself these questions:

- Is this information I need to retrieve in the future (warranties, family information, health records, etc.)?
- Is there another way I can get this information instead of filing this piece of paper?

- Do I need to save this for taxes?
- Is it reference information I need to keep?
- Is this a coupon I will use?
- Is this a receipt I need to keep?
- Is this contact information for people I associate with that I need (i.e., phone numbers and addresses that aren't kept near the phone).
- Do I need to take action? (Is this a bill to pay or do I need to RSVP for an event?)
- What will happen if I don't keep this piece of paper?

Get rid of as much as you can. Everything you keep will need to be filed.

Sort the "keeper" papers into piles such as: to read, action now, memorabilia, bills to pay, receipts, interesting things (invitations, promotional info that you need and will use), or information you have requested. Clip each pile together with a large office clip or rubber band and then stack the piles in an empty basket to be filed later.

Filing

The purpose of a working filing system is to be able to have a place for every piece of paper in your home that you can access in ten seconds or less. Only keep papers you will need to reference again, and only keep papers you can't access in an electronic manner. We'll start by setting up the system.

Here's what you will need to set up the Lights On Filing System:

1. recycle bin/bag and a trash can
2. shredder or pair of scissors
3. file cabinet (if you have a desk with file drawers, these rarely have enough room for all files but they can be used for the active files)
4. hanging files—heavy file folders with little metal hooks on both ends of the file that let the file rest on rods in the file cabinet. (These files should come with clear plastic tabs you can insert labels into. If the folders you

purchase don't have clear tabs, purchase them. The colored tabs are too hard to see through. Recycle the colored tabs. I know, it seems like a waste, but you'll be happy you did.)

5. five or six manila file folders (You probably won't need many of these as you file almost everything directly into the hanging folders. It costs less, and papers don't become lost or mixed up when using only the hanging folders.)

6. a black felt-tip marker or pen to label your files or print them on the computer. (Most computers have a word processor program that will let you create and print labels.)

7. five different colored sheets of cardstock paper (this is for creating tabs.)

The Lights On Filing System

The Lights On Filing System is color-coded to help you find exactly what you need in a matter of seconds. Files are assigned a category, and each category is assigned a specific color. All files will fit into one of five different color categories. Below are suggestions of categories and colors for that category and what to file in each category:

Red—Action/Active: Paper that requires action within the month, such as bills to pay, time-sensitive material, projects, receipts, correspondence, and coupons. You can also make folders for follow-up for papers requiring action on certain days of the month. Label these folders as follows: Days 1–8, Days 9–15, Days 16–23, Days 24–31, and Future. The Future folder is used when you receive something in one month that is happening in an upcoming month (such as a wedding invitation). Make a note of the activity in your planner or on your calendar and then file the actual paper in the Future folder (or throw it away, it is your choice). At the beginning of the new month, look in the Future file and separate what is in there by putting everything in the "dates" folders. Each of these examples will have their own file in the color red.

Green—Ongoing Resources: For example: credit history, birthday lists, home inventory, wallet contents, transit schedules, safe/storage list, health club or other agreements, associations, finances (bank statements, credit card statements, pay stubs, etc.), and other personal papers where the information changes from time to time. Each of these examples will have their own file in the color green.

In this section, information constantly changes, so when you get a new agreement, credit history, bank statement, etc., shred the old and put the new information in that folder. By constantly purging your files, you won't need to spend hours bringing your files up to date.

Orange—Specific Information Needed for Future Reference: For example: warranties and manuals (make a separate folder for each warranty or your file will be too big). Some warranties you may have are: kitchen, computer, furniture, appliance, miscellaneous warranties, and tools. When filing a manual, if there are languages you don't read, tear these pages out and recycle them to save space in your files. Staple the pages that you are keeping together. Other papers that can go in orange folders include auto titles, auto service/repair records, certificates, education records, loan history, medical records, pet records, memories/letters. Each of these examples will have their own file in the color orange.

Blue—Taxes: File past year tax returns and current year tax information. Each of these examples will have their own file by year in the color blue. Tax returns are to be kept for seven years. For more information go to www.irs.gov.

Purple—Resource Information: For example: health and fitness information, travel information, home decorating ideas, household hints, humor or gardening tips. Each of these examples will have their own file in the color purple.

I gave just a few examples of what you might label your folders. You can have as many folders appropriately labeled in each of the five categories that you need.

Label tabs in each (color) category to reflect each subject/paper you are filing. Once you've got your tabs labeled and placed on the folders, you can start placing

When to Dispose of Paperwork

Not sure how long to hold on to papers? Here are some guidelines:

- **Utility bill statements can be discarded after one month as long as you verify your payment either online or with your check or credit card statement or the current month's statement showing the previous month's payment.**
- **Pay stubs only need to be kept generally for one to three months. Depending on your employer, you may need to keep them for one year to compare your earnings for the year with your end-of-year records.**
- **Bank statements do not have to be filed, if you have access to them online. If you have paper copies consider how often you refer back to them. If you never refer to them, then why are you getting them, and why are you filing them? Do you really need to keep them in this age of computers?**

papers in each folder (after you do the next step of sorting your lose papers). I recommend you start inserting your tabs on the folders going from the left to right, staggering them so you can read each tab when they are filed in the file drawer. You can place five across before starting over again on the left side. When you come across a paper you haven't made a file for, make a new label and insert it into a folder.

Start with the loose papers you gathered from around the house. Remember to keep your shredder and recycling bin handy. Just because you've kept a paper doesn't mean you have to file it. If you won't look at the paper again, or you can find it somewhere else (like on the Internet), get rid of it. Set your timer for thirty minutes to one hour and start filing. When the thirty minutes is up, take a five-minute break and then return to filing or stop for the day and schedule a time to finish later.

Start by sorting the loose papers into the five categories (colors) you've set up. Group like papers together; for example, in the ongoing resources (green) category, gather all pay stubs in one pile, all bank statements in another pile, etc. After you have sorted your papers into piles start filing them into the appropriate folder. When you put your files in your drawer, keep each color category together. Then when you need to find a file, you will know exactly which part of the drawer your file will be in because you'll know what colored section to look for. Then you only need to thumb through the files in that category to find your specific file. For example, if you need to look at a warranty, you will know you need to look in the orange section to find it. Your mind will key in faster on where to find a paper when the paper is color coded.

Remember to evaluate all of the papers before you place them in a file. Do you really need to keep it? Be ruthless with yourself. The less you file, the more space you will have and the more time you will save now and later.

Tip: Try to limit your resource files to the fewest possible. With today's technology, it is so easy to get current information off the Internet. You'll save time and space by not filing away information you can find online.

Do not have a file labeled miscellaneous! If it is important enough to keep, it is important enough to have a specific file so you can find it.

Ninety-nine percent of the time, you only file in hanging folders. It is not often that you need to use manila folders inside the hanging folder. It costs more to buy both folders, it takes up more space to use both, and having folders inside folders can hide the folders' tabs. It also takes longer to retrieve what you are looking for.

When to File

If it is convenient to file every day, then do it. If you find it is not convenient for you, place your "to be filed papers" in a basket and schedule a time to file once a week or every two weeks at the most. It will take less than ten minutes if you file on a regular basis. If you choose to file once a week, contain all of your papers in a "to file" basket instead of scattering them around the house.

Here's an example of when to use manila folders inside a hanging file: If you have several banks but not a lot of paperwork from any of them and you don't want to make a hanging file for each institution, you could label a folder "Banks." Then within that folder use a separate manila folder for each separate bank. Or if you belong to several associations and you don't want a separate file for each one, use a manila folder for each association and put them in the hanging folder labeled "Associations." Do this only if a paper clip won't work to keep them separated.

If you currently pile your papers on top of a flat surface, my bet is you can't find them in just a few seconds. I recommend getting used to using a filing system. However, if you feel panicked at the idea that you can't visually see your papers stacked on a flat surface, then I have a solution for you: Use the colored filing system I described on pages 168–169 and place the action files (red) in a vertical slot organizer and place this on your desk. Or you can put labels on the vertical organizer for each slot and just place your papers in the slot. (Labels could be bills to pay, time sensitive, projects, coupons, and so forth.) This way you can see each paper and it will be a visual reminder of things that need to be done. Use the vertical file only for active files (red) that need action within the month. The rest of your file categories (green, orange, blue, and purple) will be filed in the filing cabinet.

Tip: Be sure to regularly update the information in your files. If you purchase a new appliance and get rid of the old appliance, toss the old manual when you file away the new one. Do the same for social security reports, insurance information, credit reports, etc. If the new information you're placing in a file makes the old information obsolete, toss the old information while you are filing the new information. Your files will stay current, and you won't have to waste time purging them.

Once you get all your loose papers filed, purge your old files and place them in new files that fit in your new system. Do this project one file at a time. Do the same thing as you did before: Evaluate the papers in the old file, separating them by category. Then sort the papers in each category, putting likes together, and create the files if you don't already have a hanging folder. Be ruthless and toss as many of the papers as possible. Shred and dispose of all papers from closed bank accounts, canceled insurance policies, canceled credit cards, and anything else you no longer need. You'll likely toss more papers than you keep. Always shred any paper with financial account numbers or social security numbers. Never toss them in the trash can.

Tip: If you have difficulty going through your files on your own, it is a good idea to ask for help from a professional organizer who is trained in filing techniques, is objective, and keeps everything confidential. It can reduce the time it takes to file and the stress involved in trial-and-error. I don't recommend a friend or family member outside your home because many files are confidential and personal.

Home Office Area

Once your filing is complete, you can create your home office area. This can be a separate room or part of another room. Keep all of your bill-paying supplies in this central location. You could keep them in the top drawer of your desk or in an attractive container with a lid that can be placed on the desk, bookcase, or table.

Place extra office supplies, such as computer paper, sticky notes, etc., in labeled containers on a shelf or in a closet in the room. Magazine holders can be used for paper, and small plastic containers are useful for other items. If you don't have a desk drawer, keep supplies like scissors, pens, pencils, and rulers in a container on the top of your desk along with tape, a stapler, and paper clips.

Keep your desktop clear. Everything kept on this surface (including papers) should be in a container (like a file or basket) so things don't get buried or lost in the shuffle of papers and create clutter.

If you don't have a designated room for a home office, you can still create a space to pay bills, file important papers, and work on your computer. If you only have a small space, an office armoire is ideal as it holds everything you need from the computer, printer, paper, pens, pencils, paper clips, and other office essentials. It is also a piece of furniture that can be used in any room in your home. A file cabinet can hold files that can be placed near the armoire or in another room if space is very limited.

A small rolltop desk is an option as it closes to hide the computer and office supplies. A two-drawer file cabinet can be placed next to it to hold files.

A designated table that holds the computer can also hold attractive containers for frequently used supplies. A file cabinet can be placed under the table to hold files. Some have smaller drawers that hold paper, pens and other supplies.

When office space is limited, it's necessary to keep the amount of paperwork you file to a bare minimum. Consider scanning documents into the computer to minimize papers in files, but be sure to have a backup system.

WRAP UP

Whew! That was a huge job and you did it! You have a system to handle mail that works for you and your family that will simplify your life and save you time.

Filing can be a daunting process, but you did it! Don't you feel fantastic now that you have purged your old files and set up a system that makes sense and works for you? Doesn't it feel good to know what is in your files and to know you can find any piece of paper in less than ten seconds?

Congratulations on:

- deciding on a landing station for all mail and containing it all in a basket or some other container
- sorting mail by asking questions to determine if you need to file it or toss it
- removing your name and address from junk mail lists
- making it a priority to go through all of the mail every day
- setting up a working filing system
- purging obsolete paperwork
- filing every piece of paper you need to keep in the appropriate folder

Now you can enjoy your new freedom from paper clutter, and it will no longer have control over your life and home. By accomplishing all of this, you must be feeling a 10 on the wattage scale!

The Craft Room or Area

(12)

Organizing your craft room (or area if you don't have a separate room) can be daunting. No matter what your crafting interest, hobbies can present storage and work-area challenges. There is a myriad of tools and supplies required for sewing and crafts activities.

An organized craft room is essential for your happiness and your ability to craft when you want to. When the area is organized, you have space to work in and still have all of your tools at your fingertips. You can effectively use the little pockets of time you find during the day to work on projects. Fifteen minutes here and there adds up to a lot of crafting time. You'll be able to complete projects at your leisure without carving huge chunks of time out of your schedule to finish projects.

SEARCHLIGHT

Walk into your craft room and use the Searchlight to take a look around. Look for the things that are working and those that aren't working for you. Take a picture of the room while you are doing your assessment. In your notebook, answer these questions:

1. What do you like about this room?
2. What is it you don't like? Identify your needs by asking yourself the following questions:
   a. What is the purpose of this room?
   b. Do you dread coming into the room because it is so messy?
   c. Is it a room you are comfortable in, and do you feel happy when you work here?
   d. Does the room encourage your creativity?
   e. Can you find the supplies you need to work on your projects? Is the space orderly?
   f. Is there sufficient room to work on projects? Do you have a table to work on?
   g. Do you need shelves, cupboards, or other containers for supplies, tools, and projects?
   h. Are your supplies organized together by craft (i.e., all scrapbooking supplies in one area, all knitting in another, etc.)?
   i. Do you have easy access to your craft tools?
   j. Are there things you can get rid of?
   k. Does everything in the room belong here? Do some items belong in other rooms?
   l. Each craft type deserves its own area (beading, scrapbooking, knitting, etc.). Are yours scattered around in different areas?
   m. Is there adequate lighting to work in?
3. Now that you have identified your needs by asking yourself these

Paula's Story

Can you relate to all or part of Paula's following experience? She used her Searchlight and immediately knew her wattage was a 2 when she tried to create something in her craft room. All her projects and supplies were scattered in different places throughout the room. The buttons, ribbons, embellishments, paper, and other supplies were jumbled together, and it was difficult to find the things she needed.

When Paula would find fifteen minutes to work on one of her projects, she would quickly head to her craft room. But she wasn't able to get anything done because she spent the entire time searching for the tools she needed for the project.

She had a lot of storage containers of all sizes, but had never used them. Her collection of books and magazines gave her inspiration for projects, and she was sure she had all the supplies she needed to create the projects, if she could just find them.

questions, use the wattage scale to rate how you feel about the room (see page 15). What is keeping you from a wattage of a 7 or above?

Once you have answered these questions and written your answers in your notebook, move on to using the Spotlight to set goals.

SPOTLIGHT

It may have been painful and a bit discouraging to identify all the problem areas in your room, but you did very well! With the Spotlight, you will focus on setting goals to transform this room into what you envision it to be so you can have a productive, organized space to craft in and a room you enjoy spending time in. You have the problem areas written down; now write down your goals. As you accomplish each one, check it off. Here are some examples of goals you could set for this room:

1. Create an orderly space by containing supplies and tools together in individual containers.
2. Create spaces for all like projects to be stored together (yarn, sewing, stamping, needlework, scrapbooking, etc., in their own designated places).
3. Clear off the table and put the items where they belong so there will be room to work on projects.
4. If you need more storage space, look for ways to create space such as installing shelves on the walls or using a bookcase.
5. Sort through the craft supplies to see if there are things you will never use or don't need and donate them. (Be honest about what you will really use as you go through this sorting process.)
6. Remove anything that doesn't belong in this room.
7. Create homes for everything in this room.
8. Add a table lamp or floor lamp to the room to improve lighting.

With your Searchlight, you probably evaluated if you have enough storage containers to properly contain all of your supplies. If you didn't, do so now. You don't necessarily need to buy new containers. Use the ones you have, and if you need more, purchase them or save money by looking around the house for more containers you can repurpose and use.

GREEN LIGHT
You have your goals and are determined to increase your wattage when you are in this room. With the Green Light, take action. Go as slowly as you need to. This room will be fun to organize, and you will find treasures you forgot you

had. When you are finished, everything will be within easy reach and accessible when you want to craft.

Stay in the Green Light and keep focused by wearing comfortable clothes, having your tool kit (see page 22), and gathering your four containers (see page 35). Get a snack and a drink.

Plan a time to start organizing in this room. Set your timer for thirty minutes to begin. You can work longer if you are in a comfortable rhythm and want to keep working. Start slowly so you don't get burned out. Part of the Green Light is to stay in the room until your planned time is up. You will get more done and have fewer distractions by staying in the room.

Start by working from the inside out. Things will definitely look worse before they look better as you will have a lot of sorting and rearranging to do.

I suggest you work in this order:

1. closet
2. cupboards and dresser or armoire
3. boxes and other containers
4. built-in shelves
5. work surfaces

Closet

Remove everything from the closet one shelf at a time. Sort through and donate or toss the odds and ends you know you'll never use again—things like short pieces of ribbon, lace, torn paper, plastic crafts you won't ever make again, the unfinished embroidery sampler you don't like anymore and don't have time to finish, paint that has dried in the tubes or bottles, paint brushes that are worn out, and other supplies you have held on to for years but have never used. This is just stuff taking up space.

As you sort, ask yourself the following questions:

- Am I saving this "just in case" I might need it someday?

- Have I considered how easily this item could be replaced if I need it in the future?
- Is this helping me create the room I want to craft in?

Continue to ask yourself these questions as you go through each shelf. Before you place things back on the shelves, determine what will go on each shelf and remember to keep like things together.

Cupboards and Dresser or Armoire

If your room has cupboards and/or a dresser or armoire that you use to store projects, organize them just as you did the craft closet. Do the same thing with each drawer as you did with the shelves, starting with the top drawer and working your way down to the bottom drawer.

If there are things that aren't in containers, put them in containers. Put your beads in small containers, scissors in another container, and sewing supplies in another area, making sure like things are kept together (thread, thimbles, needles, sewing machine attachments, etc.).

Have a place for everything and, after using the item, put it back in its place. This will make your room more efficient, and you will enjoy the time you spend crafting in your room.

Keep your tools in containers that are easy to carry to your worktable or wherever you are working on your project. By having everything within easy reach, you will save the time and frustration of hunting for what you need. Label your shelves so you will know where to return things. Get in the habit of always putting tools back where they came from as soon as you have finished using them.

Putting things back will be much easier as each item will have its own "home" within a larger container. You'll only have to take the one large thing (the container) back to the cupboard, drawer, or shelf rather than six or so small odds and ends.

Organizing Ongoing Projects

You don't always need to put a large, ongoing project away and out-of-sight if you work on it frequently. For example: A knitting project can be contained in a basket or another container. Keep the yarn, pattern, and needles in this one container that can be carried to other places to be worked on.

As you work on any large project, there will be a lot of supplies out that you will be using. To save time and to make it easier to put things away after the project is completely finished, keep like things together while working on the project. For instance, when scrapbooking an album, separate the photos into envelopes and write on the outside the date, the activity, or the city where they were taken—categorizing them in the way you are planning on putting them into your album. Keep paper in one area on your table. If you keep it in a container, it keeps it from being scattered all over. Place pens in one area, and embellishments in another. Using small containers keeps the supplies from getting lost as you are working.

This system applies to any project. Keep like things together, and when necessary, keep items in containers.

When you are through for the day or the time you have allotted to work on a project, always take time to tidy up the space. If you are coming back to the project the next day, and you don't have a room where you can close the door, but it bothers you to see your supplies out, cover the table with a cloth. This will hide the supplies and keep things just the way you left them.

If you are not going to work on the project for a few weeks, put things away so they don't get scattered around and lost. Schedule time to work on projects you enjoy doing.

Boxes and Other Containers

Open every box and all containers in your room even if you think you know what is in them. Take everything out so you can see everything in the boxes or containers. You may be surprised at what you find. As you put the things back evaluate if you want to keep them here or store them someplace else.

Built-In Shelves

Take everything off the shelves one shelf at a time if there are a lot of supplies and containers. Wipe the shelves with a cloth before putting things back. If there are not many things on the shelves you can remove everything from every shelf all at one time. As you replace the things on the shelves ask yourself the same questions you did when you were organizing the shelves in the closet.

Establish a specific home for all of your supplies and label the shelves to help you remember where to return them after you are finished using them.

Work Surfaces

Declare your work table a free zone—free of clutter that is. It is only to be used when you are crafting. Everything else goes where it belongs; magazines and books used as resources go on shelves or in magazine containers that are labeled or stacked in a basket. All tools and other supplies are in their containers where they belong unless they are being used.

Place a floor lamp or table lamp by your work or sewing table to increase the lighting. A full spectrum light is nice as it mimics natural light.

Additional Storage Options

If you don't have enough storage space for your needs, create space by installing shelves on the walls, or utilize a bookshelf. To hide a couple of shelves, buy short curtains and hang them from an extendable rod. Hang the rod towards the bottom part of the shelf (to cover the last shelf or two) by extending it from one side of the bookshelf to the other; this will hide the contents on these shelves. Clear plastic boxes are great for organizing ribbon, thread, pom-poms, sewing supplies, stencils, and hundreds of other supplies. Separate and contain matching supplies in plastic bins, using the correct size for the items.

You can attach a peg board to the wall to keep supplies within sight and easy reach. The peg board can be painted to match the wall. Spools of thread can be placed on the peg board, along with scissors, rulers, or paper that is hung from large office clips. Ribbon or rickrack can be wound around spools or hung from large office clips and hung on the peg board as well. Or, if you want to keep them in a more discrete place, these supplies can be hung from a peg board or hooks attached to the inside of the closet door.

Bookshelves can hold fabric as well as embellishments for scrapbooking. Plan to have a balance between having all the craft tools and items out on shelves and in cupboards. Too many things on open shelves can create a cluttered look. If open shelves are your only option, one way to minimize a cluttered look is to have matching bottles, baskets, and containers for all your supplies. Make sure anything kept behind closed doors can be reached and returned easily.

> **Tip:** *After you are finished crafting for the day, spend ten to fifteen minutes tidying up your work area. Put away all of your supplies and tools. Set a goal to leave your room clean and organized. The next time you work on the craft, you will be more motivated to start again, and you will feel you are starting fresh. Everything will be in its proper place, and you'll be able to find your supplies.*

Tips on Storing Fabric

Making stacks of folded fabric is fun and easy. It saves space and you can see what you have with just a glance.

Place folded fabric with the selvage to your left, and the fold on your right. A 6" × 24" (15cm × 61cm) ruler is a great tool to help you fold your fabric nicely.

When to Stop Buying

You do not need to keep buying crafting supplies just for the sake of buying them. Do not buy another tool or supply if: you already have a similar tool; you don't have enough storage space; you are buying the item simply because the store carries it; or you know you have the same item at home somewhere but can't find it.

You will save time, money, and space by keeping on-hand items you need and use and by not excessively or compulsively buying new craft items. Compulsive shopping may be one reason your room became so disorganized.

You can use any size of ruler to fold your fabric. If you have small pieces, use a narrower ruler (a 4" × 12" [10cm × 30cm] ruler works well). For ½-yard (46cm) pieces, use a 6" (15cm) or 6½" (17cm) ruler. Lay the ruler on the fabric extending from the selvage to the fold. Start folding by flipping the ruler over and over until you get to the end. Fabric should be snug but not tight. If it doesn't come out evenly, fold the last few inches back on top of the fabric.

Slide the ruler out and fold the folded end (which is on your right) to the selvage end two or three times. Now you can stack the fabric in a bin or directly on your shelves.

Separate fabric by color and size. As you are organizing your fabrics, if there are some you absolutely know you will never use because you dislike them for some reason, now is the time to donate them. I know fabric stashes are almost sacred to quilters, so let the stash work for you by keeping it organized so you know what fabric you have. Fabric can be stored on shelves so air can circulate, or stored in wire bins that are placed on shelves or in a plastic cart with drawers. Clear plastic bins can be used for storage if you don't live in an area with high humidity. Plastic "sweats" and can ruin fabric that is stored in plastic for years. To protect fabric from light, place it in a cupboard or on shelves that are out of the direct light. Fabric is pretty good at surviving intact for years, but the cooler and drier the storage environment the better.

WRAP UP

Don't you feel great creating a room that is orderly and that you feel comfortable and happy in? Having a place where you can find all your craft supplies without wasting time looking for your tools and materials creates a wattage of 10 when you walk in this room. Look at your before photo and take an after photo. Doesn't the change feel great?

Congratulations on completing the following:

- You can walk in your room and create or work on a craft project at any time.
- Your supplies are stored together by the type of craft.
- You have easy access to your craft tools.
- You sorted through all your supplies and got rid of the bits and pieces you will never use but were hanging on to.
- By using all sizes and types of containers, you can find anything you want or need in a few seconds.
- Everything in this room enables you to create; things that don't belong here have been removed.
- You have grouped like items together: fabric, yarn, bead supplies, scrapbook supplies, and other craft items.
- Everything has a home, and you will put all items back where they belong after using them.
- You have improved the lighting to make it easier to work in your room.

13

The Laundry Room

In the days of wringer washers, laundry used to be an all-day chore. Skill and timing was involved to avoid getting fingers caught in the wringer apparatus. Now it is so simple we don't always have one specific day to do laundry.

We have the convenience of washers and dryers that let us toss in the clothes with soap and softener, and then leave us free to do something else while our clothes are being washed and dried. So why is laundry such a nightmare? Let's conquer it once and for all.

SEARCHLIGHT

Start by looking for things in your laundry room that are working for you and those that aren't working for you. Write these down in your notebook. What is keeping you from a wattage that lights you up when you're in your laundry room?

1. What do you like about the laundry room or laundry area?
2. What don't you like about this room or area? Identify needs by asking yourself the following questions:
    a. Are laundry supplies organized in a way that makes it easy for you to do the laundry?
    b. Do you have space for laundry supplies, and are they easily accessible?
    c. Does your family help by bringing their clothes to the laundry area?
    d. Are there laundry baskets or hampers easily accessible in the bedrooms, bathrooms, or laundry room?
    e. Do you get the clothes folded in a timely manner?
    f. Do you have a designated time and place to fold laundry?
    g. Are family members responsible for returning clean clothes to their rooms?
    h. What else is kept in this room? Do you use this area for general storage? Is everything properly contained and organized so you can find it?
3. Now that you have taken a good look at your laundry area, rate your wattage (see page 15). Are you lit up at a 7 or above when you are in this room or space?

Once you have answered these questions and written your answers in your notebook, take a photo of this room or area for a before-and-after comparison. Now move on to the Spotlight step to set goals.

Tip: *After washing particularly dirty items, like the cat bed or really dirty, greasy clothes, sanitize your washer. Fill the machine with hot water to the maximum level, add one cup of bleach and run it for a full cycle without any clothes.*

SPOTLIGHT

With the Spotlight, you will focus on setting goals to make it easier for you to do laundry and get it put away. You wrote down the problem areas, now write down your goals. Here are some examples of goals you could set for this room or area:

1. Laundry supplies will be conveniently located. Smaller items will be contained in containers.
2. Counter space in the room will kept uncluttered and free to fold clothes.
3. Laundry baskets or hampers will be placed in convenient places throughout the house.
4. A time will be scheduled when laundry will be folded.
5. Children will be taught to do their own laundry.
6. Each family member will be responsible for returning folded clothes to his or her room.
7. Other items stored in the room will be in containers and organized in the cupboards or on shelves.

GREEN LIGHT

Your goals are set. You now have the Green Light to take action. Gather your tool kit (see page 22) and four containers (see page 35; replace the recycling container with a "mending" container). Get a drink and a snack in case you need it. You are all set to turn up the wattage in your laundry room or area.

Schedule a time to start working. Plan a specific amount of time and set your timer. When your timer rings, if you aren't finished and have the energy and are

Paula's Story

Paula disliked doing the laundry because she didn't like all the mess in her laundry room, and her family members complained that it was difficult for them to reach the laundry supplies. She used her Searchlight and Spotlight and then moved into the Green Light to make changes. She changed into shorts and a T-shirt, got a treat and a bottle of water. With her goals written in her notebook, she set her timer for forty minutes and started to make changes.

First she put together a new hamper that was divided into three sections to make sorting clothes easier for her family. Next, she picked up the clothes off the floor and sorted them by color and started a load of wash. She moved her laundry soap and dryer sheets down to a lower shelf to make them easier to reach. The new basket she had bought gave her a fun place to keep small supplies, such as stain sticks and spot treaters.

> Use a timer to help you work. If you are in a good rhythm and have the time, reset your timer when it runs out.

On the wall, she hung a hook for the broom. She swept the floor and put her new rug down. She cleared off the counter she would now use to fold clothes. She used her BE basket to hold items that belonged in other rooms rather than leaving the room. When the timer rang, she was surprised at all she had already accomplished.

She had a few more things she wanted to do so she set her timer again and had reached her goals before it rang the second time.

She felt so good to have all her goals accomplished. Now when she walks in the room, she lights up to an 8.

in a comfortable rhythm, set your timer again and keep going. When you need to take a break, set your timer for five minutes so you will remember to come back.

Start working from the inside out. It will look worse before it looks better. I suggest you work in this order:

1. top cupboards
2. bottom cupboards
3. open shelves
4. countertop
5. hamper

Use the containers you have labeled to get rid of things you don't want in this room, and don't leave the room until your timer rings.

Top Cupboards

Start with the cupboard you find most convenient for storing frequently used laundry supplies. Take everything out shelf by shelf. Wipe the shelves clean. When you put the supplies back, place them so they are the most convenient for you when you reach to use them. Contain small items like spot treatments in a basket to keep everything contained in one handy place.

Move to a different shelf and, again, remove everything from it. When you put things back, organize like things together. Continue doing this with every shelf and cupboard. When you find something that does not belong in this room, put it in the BE basket. Do not leave the room or area to take these things where they belong at this time; do that after you are completely finished in this room.

Bottom Cupboards

These can be used for items you want to store that are used on a weekly or monthly basis. Possible items could be wrapping paper, a small tool box, vases, extra paper towels, etc. If you do use the laundry room as a semi-storage room, have a place for everything that is to be stored here.

Make Laundry Easier

Do you enjoy doing laundry? You're not alone if you don't. Here are some ideas that can help make doing laundry easier.

- **Teach your children how to do their own laundry as soon as they are capable. Depending on the child, age eight to ten is a good age to teach them how to wash and fold their laundry, but you can start as early as age two by playing a game with them to find matching socks when folding clothes.**
- **Post a stain chart on the wall for older children to refer to when they need to treat a stain.**
- **Have three hampers (or one hamper with three dividers) for dirty clothes—one for whites, one for light colors, and one for darks.**
- **Keep clothespins in a basket on the counter. Family members can clip them to stains on their clothes so they can be properly treated.**
- **Interact with family members or listen to music while you fold your laundry to make the task more enjoyable.**

Has your laundry room become a catchall room? Do you or your family just chuck things in here because you don't know where else to put them, and then they stay? If this is the case, refer back to the goals you set when using the Spotlight. If items are being tossed in here that need to be stored here, make room for them and give them a home. The premium spaces in this room are at eye level or just below (see page 24). It is where the items you use most often are kept as it is the easiest and most convenient places for the laundry supplies. In the secondary spaces, keep things you use about once a week, such as paper supplies or extra cleaning supplies, and make a place for them. If you use this room for semi-storage for things such as vases, wrapping paper (not Christmas), and tools, make a place for them and label the area so your family knows where to return them. This is not the room to use for hard-core/long-term storage.

Countertop

Create as much counter space for folding clothes as possible. Whatever is on the countertop, take it off and put the items away in the cupboards, trash, mending basket, or BE basket. When the counter is kept free of clutter, it will be easier to fold clothes, and it will be an inviting room to be in.

Hamper

If there is enough room, consider having three hampers in the room (or one divided hamper)—one for whites, one for light colors, and one for dark colors. If there is room for just two hampers, use one for whites and one for colors. The dark colors and the lighter colors can be separated before washing.

If there are hampers, baskets, or laundry bags in the children's rooms, have them be responsible for bringing their clothes to the laundry room on a certain day you specify. If they don't bring their clothes to the laundry room, don't go and get them. They will run out of clothes to wear, and this will teach them the importance of helping with the laundry. Keep the supplies they will need where they can reach them.

Clothes in the Hamper or on the Floor

Sort through the clothes and put them in the appropriate section in the hamper. Treat the clothes that have stains and put the ones that need repairing in the mending basket. As you are looking at each one, donate the ones that are too small for anyone in your home to wear. (Wash all clothing items before you donate them.) Those that are ripped and stained beyond repair should be thrown away. You can start a batch of laundry right now if you want.

Tip: If the light in the room isn't bright, consider adding a full-spectrum light to make checking for stains easier.

Folding and Putting Away Laundry

After the clothes are washed, one of the biggest problems is folding all the clean clothes and getting them put away. Here are some ways to get the laundry folded before it becomes insurmountable:

1. Fold each load as it comes out of the dryer.
2. Assign one or two family members the responsibility of folding the clothes each week; rotate this task weekly.
3. When the children do their own laundry, have them be responsible to wash, fold, and put away their clothes.
4. Plan to fold the clothes in the evening during down time while watching television, or when you are supervising homework or listening to music or an audio book.
5. If you wash laundry every day, try to fold the clothes on the same day so they don't end up in piles as large as Mount Everest.
6. Place baskets on the shelves, one for each family member. Teach family members that they are responsible to take their clothes to their rooms and put them away, and to return the basket to the shelf in the laundry room. If you step in and take their clothes to their rooms for them, charge the children money when you are performing this maid service for them. It may motivate them to cooperate, and they will see you are serious. If they don't have money of their own, assign them other tasks so they can work off the charge.

This is the room where the iron and ironing board are used most often (unless you keep yours in your sewing area). Set the ironing board up against a wall so it is always convenient for ironing and pressing clothes. If space is at a premium, here are two space saving options: Use an ironing board that hangs from the back of a door or install one in the wall that folds down for use and folds back into the wall when not in use.

WRAP UP

Congratulations on using the Searchlight to pinpoint what needed to be changed, then using the Spotlight to set goals to make changes, and then using the Green Light to make your laundry room just as you want it to be.

Here is a list of things to continue to do to make doing the laundry easier:

- All laundry supplies will be located in convenient areas.
- The counters will remain uncluttered as everything will have a home and after an item is used it will be returned to its place.
- A divided laundry basket (or multiple baskets) will be used to reduce time sorting clothes.
- A specific time and place will be scheduled to fold laundry.
- Family members will be taught to do their own laundry when they are old enough.
- Each family member will be responsible for returning folded clothes to their rooms to put them away.
- Items stored in this room will be contained and neatly organized in the cupboards or on the shelves.

With your organized laundry room or space, it will be easier to do the laundry, and with everyone in the home helping, it will no longer be a hassle to wash, dry, fold, and put away the laundry.

Downsizing

(14)

If you have ever considered downsizing, this chapter is for you. It focuses on downsizing for a move, but you can downsize even if you aren't planning to leave your current home. If you start the downsizing process before you actually need to move, you will have the time you need to adjust to the idea of moving. Reducing the amount of your possessions on a regular basis will help you avoid the physical exertion and emotional trauma of doing it all at once.

Do you find yourself living in a home that has become too large for you? Have you started thinking about downsizing, but you aren't sure you want to leave your home? Or, would you like to move but are afraid if you get rid of your belongings you will be letting go of your memories? This chapter can help you find peace.

SEARCHLIGHT

With your Searchlight, ask yourself the following questions to help you decide if it is time to downsize to move to a different home. Write down your answers in a notebook. What wattage do you feel? On a scale of 1 to 10 do you have the feeling of 7 or above as you ask yourself these questions?

For Homeowners:

1. What do you love about living in your house?
2. Can you afford to keep the house?
3. Will the house need major work in the next few years (e.g., new roof, furnace, etc.)?
4. Have the stairs become a problem for you? Do you worry about falling?
5. Is the house too big for your needs?
6. Are you able to keep up with the daily maintenance?
7. Has the yard become a burden?
8. Can you keep up with the housekeeping? (Can you bend down to clean up spills so they aren't a hazard?)
9. Do you feel you can stay in your home, but you have too many things to take care of and it consumes too much of your time?
10. Are your children or relatives storing their things in your home?
11. Are there adequate community resources that you can easily access (i.e., health care, shopping, and public transportation)?
12. Has the neighborhood changed, or is it no longer safe to live in?
13. Are you isolated from friends and family in your home?
14. Would you like to live closer to your adult children and grandchildren?
15. Are you able to take care of your medical needs in your current home (e.g., taking medications on time, diabetes testing, etc.)?
16. Make a list of your housing needs and desires. Can these be satisfied with other housing?
17. Do you feel you can continue to live in your home with some

Relocating for Older Adults

Relocating can be a traumatic experience for anyone, but it is especially so for older adults and their adult children. Children who live close by may feel they are asked to do too much, and those living far away may feel guilty because they aren't closer to help in the process. However, with good planning, much of the frustration and trauma can be avoided.

Many seniors contemplating moving from their homes may see it as the beginning of the end. However, it can be a wonderful time for seniors as there are many opportunities for easier and better living after moving from a house that has outgrown them. There are many options, such as comfortable condominiums, gated communities, retirement centers, assisted care centers, or "mother-in-law apartments."

professional assistance as needed (e.g., housekeeping, Meals on Wheels, activities through a senior citizens center that also picks you up for activities, etc.)?

18. If you wait too long, will someone else have to make the decision to move for you?

19. What will you gain by moving into a retirement community or assisted living? Have you considered the following?

    a. staff to check on your health and security

    b. housing that is private, clean, and on one level if needed

    c. Provided meals (either part or all), which eliminates shopping, cooking, and washing dishes

Paula's Story

Paula was very concerned about her elderly parents staying alone in their family home for several reasons. Her father would forget to take his medications, and when encouraged to take them, he would become angry and accuse her mother of treating him like a child.

They had been taken advantage of by a man who had come to their door saying their roof needed repairing. Being trusting people, they gave him several thousand dollars for repairs and never saw him again.

Her mother's vision was starting to decline, and when something was spilled on the floor, she didn't see it and she slipped and fell. The laundry room was in the basement, and Paula knew it was hard for her parents to go up and down the stairs to do their laundry.

Her mother drove her father to his doctor's appointments but her reflexes, as well as her vision, weren't as good as they used to be, and Paula feared her mother would cause a car accident.

Socially, her parents were isolated. Their friends and family had moved away. They wanted to go out and do fun activities but they didn't have anyone to go with, and her mother couldn't drive at night.

Paula thought it would be hard for her parents to leave the home they had lived in for thirty years. She expected resistance when she talked to her parents about moving, and she was prepared to let the idea of downsizing and moving to a smaller home sit with them for a while. She was surprised that they actually were eager to move to a different place with less upkeep and where they could be around others their own age. They had wanted to move but were afraid their children would not want them to leave the family home.

d. convenient medical services

e. other seniors that live close who have the same interests and provide a social network for activities

Does downsizing and moving make you feel anxious? It does for the majority of people who are moving. Even if you decide not to move, just think of how much you'll gain by getting rid of years of accumulated clutter. You will have more freedom, more space, and feel happier and be more peaceful in your home. When the time does come for you to move to a different place, you will have done yourself and your family a favor by sorting through everything before it has to be done. A great gift to leave your heirs is to sort and clear out your belongings so they don't have to do it after you are gone.

For Adult Children

1. Is there someone who lives near your parents who can monitor and assist them when they need it?

2. Are you willing to agree to let your parents downsize according to their schedule, needs, and wishes?

3. Have you cleaned out all of your belongings from your parents' attic, basement, or garage (e.g., old school papers, sports memorabilia, wedding dress, photo albums, scrapbooks, dolls, card collections, etc.)?

4. Have you given your parents permission to toss out or give away any gift that you have given them (like the clay pot you made in the sixth grade)? Let them know you are happy with them parting with anything you have given them if they no longer need, want, or have space for it. This will release them from feeling guilty and allow them to let go.

SPOTLIGHT
After using your Searchlight to ask yourself questions about downsizing, you wrote the answers in your notebook, and possibly discussed it with your family; now it is time to use the Spotlight to make some goals.

Downsize Through Gift Giving

Heather's grandparents gave family heirlooms and treasures to their grandchildren for special occasions long before they planned to move from their home. It gave them pleasure to see how much their grandchildren enjoyed their gifts. They also shared their memories about each item as they gave them to the children. This method allowed them to downsize a little at a time. When they passed away, there were very few things of either monetary or sentimental value left in their home. Living on a fixed income, they also saved money by sharing their treasures. And there was no fighting within the family as to who would get what when the grandparents passed away.

Possible goals could be:

For Homeowners:

1. Make the decision to downsize and move while you can and before an illness or an injury makes the decision for you later. This could force you to move when you aren't ready.
2. Take inventory of everything in your home and decide what you want to do with those belongings.
3. Hire a professional organizer to help with the downsizing process.
4. Hire professionals who specialize in working with seniors.
5. Hire a real estate agent to help locate a house that fits your needs. Visit retirement centers and other places you think you might like to move to.
6. Downsize and stay in your home.

For Adult Children: If you feel your parents should move and they don't want to, work to support them in their decision. You can help arrange for service providers to come into their home if that is what they need.

Respect their desires and continue to be encouraging, not nagging. When role reversal happens parents may resent their children taking over. Encourage them to downsize even if they plan to stay in their home.

GREEN LIGHT

Once you have set your goals and made the decision to downsize, start with one room at a time. As with the other rooms in your home, start working from the inside out. Look in drawers one at a time, then the closets, armoires, and next on shelves to see what you have that you want to get rid of, either by giving to someone else, recycling, donating to charity, tossing, or selling. During the downsizing process, start slow. At first, it may be hard to let go of things, but as the idea "takes root" and you realize it is okay to let go of a few things, it will be easier to let go of more. It does not have to be traumatic or exhausting to downsize if it is done a little at a time.

Consider the amount of space you will have in your new home and plan accordingly. Chances are, you have collected many things during the years, and you will need to be selective of the items you can move.

Before you start, take photos of every room in your home and the treasures you cherish. Put the photos in a special photo album. After the move, when you look through them, they will bring back memories.

Set your timer for twenty minutes to an hour when you start any project. This will help prevent burnout and keep you from getting too tired when sorting through your belongings. Always think of others as you sort and ask yourself who you want to give the item to, what charity could benefit from it, or whether it is worn out and it is time to throw it away or recycle it.

Sort belongings into three categories.

1. *Keep:* Things that will be moved to your new home.
2. *Give away:* Things that will be given to family, friends, and charity or be sold.
3. *Toss:* Things that aren't of use to anyone and need to be discarded.

For further information on how to sort and downsize, refer to the chapters in this book dealing with the particular room you are working in.

If you have treasures (figurines, photo albums, mementos from travels, jewelry, books, and other items) that you can't part with right now, but you want them to go to certain people, write a description of each item in a notebook and put it with your trust or will so those people will get them at the appropriate time.

Consider giving these items to those people now so you can enjoy seeing them receive the gift and the happiness and joy you have brought into their lives by sharing with them. You can share with them the stories attached to each item.

Even before you have secured your new home or living arrangement, start sorting and packing. It may be necessary to hire a professional to help with this, or get help from friends and family.

Arrange to sell or donate cars and furniture, meet with the movers, take photos of possessions, and interact with family members who are helping with the move. Assign someone to arrange for auctions, estate sales, and antique appraisals if needed. All of these tasks can also be done by a professional who is knowledgeable about the special needs of seniors.

If you decided to downsize and stay in your home, begin to sort through your possessions. Take your time. Sometimes it takes organizing the things you have collected before you can decide what to keep or give away.

Photos and memorabilia and what to do with them will be discussed in Chapter 15.

WRAP UP

You have made the decision to downsize whether you chose to move or to stay in your own home. You will have a successful downsizing process by:

- Designating how you will give away or pass along the treasures you love. If you are keeping them but want to designate who will inherit them when you no longer want them, place a label in an inconspicuous place on the items to make your desires known. Or write the description of the item along with the name of the person who will receive it and put it with your will and trust.
- Starting to give your children their "inheritance" now. Enjoy this time with them as they go through the family treasures and select what they want.
- Using technology to digitally save photos and other paper memorabilia. Or have someone in your family help you to put together a scrapbook of your life.
- Not holding on to clutter. You will enjoy the benefits of living in a well organized home.

Downsizing and sharing your belongings and limiting yourself to what you need and love will enrich your life and the lives of others.

Memorabilia and Inherited Items

Is your home full of inherited items and memorabilia that you just don't know what to do with—important things like photos, cards, letters, knickknacks, furniture, linens, kitchen items, and personal items? The things we hold onto can remind us of family, special places we have visited, and other memories. We sure do have a love affair with our photos, old letters, and other memorabilia. However, these things can also create clutter, take up valuable space, and cause all sorts of problems.

Are these things taking up valuable space in your home that you would rather be using for other things? Do you spend too much of your time taking care of these inherited items or old memorabilia? Has it crossed the line from being treasures to being trash? You are not alone! Help is here.

Dawn's Story

Can you relate to Dawn? Dawn was at her wits end. She inherited a garage full of boxes and furniture from her parents. She lived in a two-bedroom condominium and had a one-car garage. Because she had to hurry and get the things out of her parents' house, everything had been crammed in her garage, and for a year it had not been touched. She was tired of not being able to use her garage. And she felt guilty not taking care of their things. She felt awful every time she had to go into her garage. For her own piece of mind, she really wanted most of the things moved out of her garage. The rest she wanted organized so she knew what was there and could enjoy it.

SEARCHLIGHT

Start with the Searchlight and take your time assessing what you have. You may have emotional feelings as you start to sort and purge, so prepare yourself. It is easier to pick up a kitchen utensil and decide what to do with it than it is to sort through years of personal belongings or those of a family member and make decisions on what to do with the items.

As you look at each item, think about what wattage are you feeling (see page 15). At a 7 or above, you are happy and feeling good. Any number under that, and you have feelings that don't light you up. If your wattage is under 7, let the item go. Identify what you want to do with inherited items or personal memorabilia by asking yourself the following questions:

1. Do you own too many things for the space you have?
2. Do you feel you are the "Keeper of Memories" for the family?

3. Why do you want to keep this?
4. Are you keeping this because it allows you to live in the past rather than the present?
5. Are you keeping it out of spite of another family member?
6. Does it bring back bad memories?
7. Is this meaningful or valuable to you? Or is it just cluttering your life?
8. Do you like it enough to want it on display?
9. Can you safely display it?
10. Would someone else benefit more by having this item either because they could use it or because they have a memory attached to it?
11. Do you want to pass this on to a family member?
12. If you store it, will you ever look at it again?
13. Do you have photos stuck in multiple boxes that you have forgotten the names of people in them and the places where they were taken? Are the photos no longer important to you?
14. Are you holding onto your adult children's baby books, trophies, and items from their childhood?
15. Do these things hold you back from what you want and need?
16. When traveling, do you buy souvenirs that just take up space and gather dust?

Once you have answered these questions and written your answers in your notebook, you can move onto the Spotlight to set goals.

SPOTLIGHT

It can be very emotional and difficult to look at things that mean a lot to you and know that they have not been honored in the way you would like them to be.

With the Spotlight, you will focus on setting goals to get your memorabilia

Paula's Story

Paula knows she has a love affair with the memorabilia she has collected through the years. She has many trinkets (stashed somewhere) from different places she has traveled, and her photos are in drawers, on the bookcase, and in boxes.

Using the Searchlight, she realized she really did want to organize her memorabilia. She used the Spotlight and came up with a few goals that would work for her. She would buy a photo album to slip the pictures in and add clear envelopes for small treasures (like a sea shell, a leaf, and a heart-shaped rock among other things). She decided to pick a day to set her timer and collect as many photos as she could find. Then she scheduled three different nights to work on putting the photos in the album. She told her family her plans and asked for their cooperation in helping her achieve her goal. They got in the spirit of things, offering to help her find the photos. She wrote this down in her notebook as one of her goals. With all of her goals written down, she was ready to step into the Green Light.

and inherited items organized so you can enjoy them. Write down your goals and, when you are in the Green Light, check off each goal as it is accomplished. Here are some examples of goals you may set:

1. Remove excess items so you cherish what is left and have room for all the items in the space available to you.

2. As the keeper of these inherited items, give items away to family members so they can be enjoyed and used. Donate the rest to charity or sell them.

3. Keep only precious, meaningful keepsakes rather than keeping everything.
4. Get rid of anything associated with bad or negative memories.
5. If anything is not meaningful or valuable to you and doesn't light you up on the wattage scale at a 7 or above, donate, toss, or recycle it.
6. Display items you truly love and care about.
7. Let go of items if there is no place to keep them.
8. If there are things that have to be stored, and you have storage space, pack them carefully and label the boxes.
9. Organize all photos by person, place, or date that you are keeping. You do not need to keep every single photo.
10. Ask someone in the family to put photos in albums for you.
11. Have your children (that no longer live in your home) take their memorabilia.
12. Only keep things that light you up and you have the space for.

> "Obstacles are what you see when you take your eye off the goal."
>
> —VINCE LOMBARDI

Write down a target date to complete these goals. Sorting and making decisions may be hard, but you can do it! Keep reading the goals you have set and think about how good you will feel when you can park in the garage (because large inherited items have been removed).

GREEN LIGHT

You have used the Searchlight to determine what is working and what is not working for you. Then you used the Spotlight and set some great goals. Now let's get down to work and move into the Green Light.

Get in the Green Light by wearing comfortable clothes and turning off the

Lou Ann's Story

Lou Ann inherited valuable jewelry, Lladró figurines, and clothing from her mother. She was offered furniture and kitchen items, but she kindly refused these items as there wasn't anything of sentimental value and she already had a household full of things she currently used and liked.

She took several pieces of the jewelry, had the stones reset, and gave one each to her children. It is a lovely reminder to them of their grandmother. Her philosophy is: "I am against storing stuff because then you can't enjoy it. Isn't that what curio cabinets are for?"

phone or letting the machine take the messages. Gather your tool kit (see page 22) and your four containers (see page 35). Set your timer for the amount of time you can devote to working on one part of the project at a time. Schedule a time to start working when you have the most energy. At first, work for thirty minutes at any one time so you don't get burned out as you start sorting through papers, old letters, gifts, souvenirs, etc. As you get into a rhythm and are more comfortable going through the boxes, you can increase the amount of time you spend organizing.

Perhaps invite a family member, friend, or professional organizer to help you sort through the boxes, papers, and other things you have collected or inherited.

Work from the inside out whenever possible—closets, drawers, shelves, and cupboards first. Start with the places that are bothering you the most. If you have a room full of inherited items, boxes, and miscellaneous items, start there. Go through one box at a time. Do not move on to another box until you have looked at the things in the box and determined where everything in that box will go.

When you are going through memorabilia that you have accumulated on your own, such as souvenirs, gifts, photos, and knickknacks, keep referring back to your goals. Be tough on yourself if you need to be. Clear the clutter and display the items you are keeping in the way you want to, while making space in your home for comfortable living.

Remember things will look worse before they look better. That is just how it is and it is okay. Things will look and feel better once you are finished.

WRAP UP

This may be one of the hardest things you have ever done in your life—organizing other people's things that you felt responsible for and organizing your personal memorabilia. You did a great job! It was sure worth it, wasn't it?

The way to keep your own memorabilia organized is:

- Do not purchase souvenirs that gather dust. Buy a T-shirt or something that you can use instead or let your photos be your souvenirs. Buy a unique cleaning product in a foreign country and every time you use it, you'll think of the time you were shopping there. Or buy a Christmas ornament, and each year you'll remember your visit.
- Only print photos that you will put in a photo book—no more loose photos. Another option is to display digital photos on a digital picture frame that scrolls to a different picture every few seconds. Put digital photos on a disk or save them on your computer in a folder labeled by date or event. Or send them to a Web site that lets you turn your photos into a hardbound book.
- Keep collections together and only keep the ones that are meaningful to you and that you have space for.
- Instead of buying more knickknacks that you will need to dust, plan to use the money some other way.

Remember, it is all just stuff. If an object lights you up and is organized, it can enrich your home and your life, and bring back great memories.

The Storage Room

(16)

Do you have a room where you store off-season decorations, extra paper products, camping gear, and other household items that you need to keep but use infrequently? It could be your attic, basement, or a spare bedroom. Do you have a place you call your storage room, but in reality it has become a junk room—a dumping ground for anything you don't know where to put? Does your family open the door and toss things into this room, and now you can't even get in it? Do you go out and buy an item even though you know you have the same item in the storage room but can't find it? If you experience any of these problems, let me show you how you can transform this room back into a functional storage room.

Paula's Story

Paula was thrilled when she bought her house because it had a large storage room. She was sure it was big enough to store everything she needed to store, from holiday decorations to things she bought in bulk.

She labeled all the plastic bins in the room. In her most recent move, she labeled each plastic bin with a number. In a notebook,

she wrote the contents of each bin to its corresponding number. (She filed this under Household in her office files.) This worked for her because she knew where to find everything she was storing until it had a permanent home.

She had organized things on shelves and had always been able to find what she needed. One day Paula was surprised when she couldn't get into the storage room. She and her family had started opening the door and tossing things in. The items on the shelves were mixed up, camping gear and unrolled sleeping bags had been thrown back in a corner, and other items weren't put back in their containers or returned to their designated places.

This room had become a dumping place for her family members when they didn't know where else to put something.

At one time, it had been a room where everything could be found easily. Paula was determined to make it meet her needs again.

SEARCHLIGHT

With your Searchlight, look in your storage room for the things that work for you and for the problem areas that aren't working for you. Write each of these things down in your notebook. Take a picture while you are assessing this room. When you are finished, you can visually see the progress you made.

1. What do you like about the room?
2. What doesn't work for you in this room? Some questions you could ask yourself to identify your needs are:
   a. What is the purpose of this room?
   b. Are there shelves to hold what is stored here? Can they be adjusted to better suit your needs? Do you need additional shelves?
   c. Are there things here that need to be in other places in the home, or donated or thrown away?
   d. Are the things you use most often easily accessible?
   e. Are things clearly labeled?
   f. Does everything have a designated place?
   g. Do items need to be repacked to make them fit on the shelves better and take up less space?
   h. Would adding cupboards to this room help you make the best use of the space?
3. You have taken a good look at this room; now rate your wattage (see page 15). Where are you on this scale? Is that where you want to stay, or do you want to feel like a 10?

> As you evaluate the room, ask yourself how it got in its current state.

Now that you have answered these questions and written your answers in your notebook, you can use the Spotlight to set goals.

SPOTLIGHT

It may have been overwhelming and even a little disturbing as you assessed your storage room, especially if you couldn't even get in it because of all the stuff that had been tossed willy-nilly in the room. You did well identifying the problem areas and coming up with ideas of what you want this room to look like and how you want it to function for you.

Now write down your goals. After you have finished organizing this room, go back and check off each goal and see how it makes you feel. Here are some examples of goals you could set for this room:

1. Install additional shelving.
2. Make better use of the shelves in the room by adjusting them, placing items in containers, and using the right-sized containers for what is being stored.
3. Install hooks on the wall to hang items to free up space on shelves and the floor. (You can hang things like sporting equipment, camping gear, and seasonal items.)
4. Place items used most often in the most convenient places. Store seasonal items so they are out of the way, yet accessible when you need them.
5. Label all containers.
6. Use containers for small items, like collections, seasonal items, candles, vases, extra cords, or electronic parts.

> Plan to organize the room when you won't encounter distractions.

Tip: Label every container, box, or bin if it is not obvious what is in it. You think you will remember what is in them, but chances are you won't. It makes it faster to find things when they are labeled.

GREEN LIGHT

You have identified the problems and have set your goals by writing them in your notebook. Let's get in the Green Light and take action.

This room will take some time to organize, so schedule a time that is convenient for you when there aren't other distractions (such as children needing your attention or others wanting your time).

Wear comfortable clothes and set your timer for at least one hour. When your timer goes off, take a break for a few minutes if you need to. Set your timer for five minutes to remind yourself to come back to the room. If you are in a good working rhythm and you have time, set your timer for another thirty minutes to one hour. If it takes more than a few hours to organize, that is OK. The key to getting it all done is to keep working until you are satisfied.

Gather your tool kit (see page 22) and four containers (see page 35). Have a drink and a snack with you. You are ready to turn up the wattage in this room and reclaim it for a storage room.

As always, work from the inside out. Here's the order I recommend you work in:

1. cupboards
2. shelves
3. storage containers

Whether you have a cupboard or shelves, take everything off, one shelf at a time, and wipe off the shelf. As you remove each item, immediately evaluate the item. Ask yourself if you use the item, like the item, and want to keep the item. Then ask if it belongs in the room. If it does, set it aside with other items like it (place all holiday decorations in a pile, all sports equipment in another, etc.). Otherwise, place the item in one of the four containers—trash, donate, recycle, or BE basket. Have a specific reason for everything you keep. If you keep something "just because" or "just in case," ask if it's really worth sacrificing storage space to keep it.

Once you've cleared all the cupboards and shelves, tackle the storage containers already in the room. You may not remember what's in them. Sort each item in each container and add it to the appropriate piles, keeping like-items together. This makes it easier to put things back and then find them in the future.

Once you've cleared all the cupboards and shelves and sorted everything, decide where you will place things. As you decide where to store things, divide the shelves and the space into premium, secondary, semi-storage, and hard-core storage.

Premium space is the space reserved for things you use most often. It is the space within easy reach—from your knees to one reach above eye level.

Secondary space is the space just beyond premium space—the higher and lower shelves. You can reach the items, but may need to bend down or get a step stool.

Semi-storage items are things that are only used once a year, like holiday decorations. These can be placed in the back of the room or on the highest or lowest shelves. It is not as convenient to reach, but you only need to reach them once a year. If you need to adjust shelves to facilitate things fitting better in all the spaces do so.

Hard-core storage is for things that only need to be opened every few years. These boxes could contain yearbooks, childhood items, memorabilia you have inherited and are passing down to other generations, or if you are storing things for your adult children who have moved out of your home.

Tip: Keep all like-items together. This makes it easier to find what you are looking for and saves time when putting things away and getting things out.

As you place things in containers, consider using colored containers for seasonal times of the year so you can quickly identify what is in them (pink for spring, black and orange for Halloween, green and red for Christmas, etc.). Clear storage containers may crack sooner in very cold weather. Heavier, more durable containers last longer in extreme temperatures.

When purchasing containers, look at them on the inside as well as the outside. Some taper in at the bottom or on the sides, so there is less storage space. Others have lids that fit even with the top of the container; others have lids that leave two or three inches above the container so you can store more in them.

Label all containers. Label shelves when necessary, so items used infrequently are put back in their place.

WRAP UP

Are you thinking: *Wow, this room sure looks good! It was a lot of work, but it feels good to have it organized.* Take a moment to enjoy how happy you are feeling. I'm proud of you. This is a room often neglected because no one outside the family normally sees it, and it is easy to put off organizing because it is not a room that is used often.

Now that your storage room is organized, how do you keep it organized?

- Have shelves to store items on.
- Designate places for everything.
- Label all containers. Label shelves when necessary, so items used infrequently are put back in their place. This works well for products purchased in bulk. When the supply is used up, there is still a place for it when you restock the item.
- Put things back in their places after using them. Teach family members to do the same.
- Every two to three months, assess if things are the way you want them. If they aren't, take a few minutes to put things back where they belong and this room will stay organized.

Congratulations on a job well done!

(17) Live It, Love It, Lights On

Now that you have a more organized life and more organized spaces and rooms, don't you feel better about yourself, your home, and your office? You will most likely save money and have more freedom now that you have an organized home. Isn't it a great feeling to be able to find everything in your home with minimum effort? Have you gotten up in the middle of the night and been able to put your finger on the medicine you needed or found something else you were looking for? Have you been away from home and explained over the phone to a family member where to find something because you knew exactly where it was?

Let's have a little review of all you've accomplished:

With each room you worked in, you first started with the Searchlight and assessed everything that worked for you and everything that didn't work. Next, you used the Spotlight and set goals helping you focus and create a wattage of a 7 or above in each room. With the third step, you were given the Green Light to implement your goals. It wasn't necessarily an easy process, but it has been worth all your effort and work. You can see the results and feel the freedom, happiness, peace, and freshness within your home and yourself. Don't you just feel lighter?

Your clutter-free porch and tidy entryway warmly welcome guests to your home. When unexpected guests come over, you can enjoy visiting with them instead of being uncomfortable about the clutter piled up everywhere.

In your kitchen, you can easily find all your supplies, and everything has a designated place. As you go room to room, you should feel proud of yourself because of all your hard work! Believe me; I am very proud of you!

Now that every room in your home is organized, you may be asking how do I keep it organized?

Honestly, I don't think it is a realistic expectation that your home will *stay* organized 100 percent of the time. Life happens, and things do get disorganized one way or another. But it's important that they don't stay that way. It is possible to *keep* organized by using each of the steps we have talked about in the previous chapters.

1. Regularly check your wattage in each room and always stay at a 7 or above.
2. If you slip below a 7, use the Searchlight in each room to identify what is working and not working for you and your family.
3. Use the Spotlight to set goals.
4. Use the Green Light to make changes and tweak things before they get out of control.

Paula's Story

Paula was happy with the progress she had made in organizing her home. Her porch was free of clutter and debris. She could walk into every room in her home and find what she needed. She felt peaceful and less stressed. She liked being in her home.

She saved money because, when she shopped, she wasn't buying duplicate things she knew she had at home but couldn't find. When she was shopping, she also considered if she had room for what she was going to buy before making the purchase.

> Organizing is an ongoing process, not a job that is done once and lasts a lifetime.

One of the things she liked best was that everything had a designated place to be—everything had a home. She had taught her family to put things back when they were finished using something. They weren't perfect, but it was much better than it was before, and they were all working on putting things away.

She realized organizing is an ongoing process and not a job that is done once and lasts a lifetime. When something was out of place, she stopped herself from thinking and feeling that everything was disorganized. With her Searchlight, she looked around and realized it was only in a few places that needed to be tweaked and brought back into order.

Paula feels good about herself and her home and the amount of time she saves not having to look for things. She is happy when she has guests drop by; she has peace of mind and energy, and she has less stress and frustration in her life. She feels rested and in control.

Stay in the Green Light

When you do enter the Green Light to update the organization in your home, these tips will help you manage and complete the project:

- **Always start slow. Take baby steps.**
- **Keep only things that you use or that light you up.**
- **Work from the inside out in every room.**
- **Eliminate distractions (e.g., the phone, young children) when working on an organizing project.**
- **Set deadlines.**
- **Use your timer.**
- **Don't keep things "just in case you may need them someday."**
- **Make use of the pockets of time you have every day to "tweak" things before clutter takes over.**

5. Have a place for everything (a home) and teach family members to put things back after use.
6. Use containers to keep things together and to make it easy to put things away after being used.
7. Use your space to your advantage; designate it as premium, secondary, semi-storage, and hard-core storage (see pages 24–25) for a full explanation of this concept).
8. Before deciding what to bring into your home and what to keep remember that whatever you do keep will take more of your time now and in the future.

Tip: *Say you have tried everything for creating a clutter-free home and you have worked hard to get it organized, but it just never comes together the way you want. Maybe you are setting expectations that are too high. If you expect your home to always look like the cover of a magazine, you're bound to be disappointed. Make sure you set goals that meet your needs and help you function better in and feel better about your home. It doesn't have to look perfect to be organized.*

I encourage you to feel the joy, pride, and satisfaction of having your home organized. You have moved toward a better, peaceful, brighter, and happier life. You can now spend more time doing the things you like to do. By having an organized home, you have peace of mind, happiness, and energy, as well as less stress and frustration in your life. You did a fantastic job. It is not always easy or pleasant to assess our problem areas and then change them, but you did it!

Appendices

The following worksheets will help you use the Searchlight and Spotlight steps. There are also examples of complete worksheets to help you determine what information to include on your own sheets. Refer to these sheets as you use the Searchlight and Spotlight around your home. Write your answers in your organizing notebook.

SEARCHLIGHT WORKSHEET (Example)

This is what Paula's Searchlight Worksheet looked like when she evaluated her laundry room.

1. Determine Wattage: _Paula rated her wattage at a 3._

2. Set the Intention: _Her intention was to raise this room to a wattage of 8. The difference between an 8 and a 10 for her is that she can simply feel comfortable in this room; it doesn't need to be a showroom. She wants it to be a room she enjoys being in, but it's the laundry room, so she doesn't have to have the finest of everything to light her up here. She wants it to be a room she enjoys going into instead of avoiding the room because it is gloomy, overwhelming, and messy._

3. Identify What Is Working: _Paula likes the clothesline in the room because she can hang clothes on it when she takes them out of the dryer. She likes the counter space to fold clothes. She likes the cubby compartments where she keeps baskets for each member of the family and that each person takes his or her basket to his or her own room when laundry is finished._

4. Identify What Isn't Working: _Paula determined what wasn't working for her were: dirty clothes all over the floor, laundry supplies that were not easy to reach, and boxes that belonged somewhere else were stored in this room. She didn't like her laundry basket. It was in good condition, but it didn't work for her. Her sister had given her the rug on the floor, and she disliked the colors. She didn't like that the counter space was always filled with clutter._

SEARCHLIGHT WORKSHEET (Photocopy for your own use.)
Use this sheet for each room in your home.

1. Check your current wattage for this room. On the wattage scale of 1 to 10 how do you feel? This is an emotional way of looking at organizing. Pay attention to how you feel in this room, not to how you logically perceive the room should look according to other people's opinions. Your goal isn't to make your home look like the pages of a magazine. Your goal is to create an environment that makes you happy and meets your everyday needs in realistic ways.

   _____

   _____

   _____

2. Set your intention for what you want your wattage to be.

   _____

   _____

   _____

3. Identify what is working for you in each room.

   _____

   _____

   _____

4. Identify what isn't working for you in each room.

   _____

   _____

   _____

SPOTLIGHT WORKSHEET (Example)

This is what Paula's Spotlight Worksheet looked like when she evaluated her laundry room.

1. Problem: _Dirty clothes all over the floor_

   Goal: _Buy a hamper with three dividers: one for whites, one for colors, and one for darks. Train each family member to put his or her clothes in the assigned spot instead of on the floor._

2. Problem: _Laundry supplies that are not easy to reach_

   Goal: _Move the laundry supplies to a lower shelf and keep all the small supplies together in a container._

3. Problem: _Storage boxes that take up space and don't belong in this room_

   Goal: _Take the storage boxes to the storage room to make more space in the laundry room._

4. Problem: _Ugly rug on the floor_

   Goal: _Replace the rug; donate this one to charity or ask her sister if she wants the rug back._

5. Problem: _Cluttered counter space that prevents her from using it to fold clothes_

   Goal: _Designate homes for everything on the counter and put things back in their homes after use so the counter will stay uncluttered. Train family members and get their support to keep this area free of "stuff."_

SPOTLIGHT WORKSHEET (Photocopy for your own use.)

In your notebook write down specific goals on how to change each thing you found that didn't work for you in each room.

Room: _____

1. Problem: _____
   Goal: _____
   _____
   _____

2. Problem: _____
   Goal: _____
   _____
   _____

3. Problem: _____

   Goal: _____
   _____
   _____

4. Problem: _____
   Goal: _____
   _____
   _____

5. Problem: _____

   Goal: _____

   _____

   _____

6. Problem: _____
   Goal: _____

   _____

   _____

7. Problem: _____
   Goal: _____

   _____

   _____

8. Problem: _____

   Goal: _____

   _____

   _____

9. Problem: _____

   Goal: _____

   _____

   _____

Index

armoires, 62, 102, 182

artwork, children's, 119-120

baskets, 20, 49
  blankets, 64, 65
  books, 117
  craft supplies/projects, 117, 183
  magazines/newspapers, 62, 141, 148
  mail, 50, 85, 86, 163
  toys, 59, 65
  See also laundry basket

bathrooms, organizing, 133, 143
  countertops, 136, 141-142
  cupboards, 138
  doing work (Green Light) 136-143
  evaluating before (Search-light), 134
  planning before (Spot-light), 135-136
  towels, 125, 126, 128, 131, 135, 138, 141

bed, storage under, 102, 103, 118, 128

belongs elsewhere (BE) basket, 35

benches/chests, 62, 102

blankets and quilts, 64, 65, 102, 130, 148, 157

books, organizing, 110, 148
  baskets, 117
  bookcases, 101, 117, 149, 153, 157
  bookshelves, 59, 62, 111, 117-118, 153, 180, 185
  containers, 123

getting rid of, 62, 118, 123, 157

boxes, 99, 181, 184
  See also Game Savers™ boxes; toys/games/puzzles, organizing

children, involving in organizing/maintaining process, 106-107, 111-114, 122, 194–197

children's bedrooms, organizing, 105–106, 122–123
  closet, 108, 110, 111, 112–114
  cubbies, 111, 112, 117
  doing work (Green Light), 111-122
  dresser, 108, 110, 111, 114-115
  evaluating before (Search-light), 106-108
  planning before (Spot-light), 108-111

closets, organizing
  hangers, 19, 96, 113
  hanging rack, 96
  hooks, 99
  rods, 95-99, 113, 123
  shelf dividers, 96
  shelves, 123

clothing and accessories, 52, 93, 96-99, 112-114
  categorizing, 97-99
  getting rid of, 52, 96-97, 102, 113, 123, 195-196
  off-season storage, 102, 103, 114

containers, 20-22, 99-100, 228

books, 123
children's artwork, 123
children's treasures, 121-122
craft supplies, 110, 117, 123, 182, 185
labeling, 19, 25, 82, 114, 117, 125, 126, 131, 154, 174, 213, 220, 223
refrigerator and freezer food, 86
school supplies, 117
See also baskets; boxes; containers, essential; toys/games/puzzles, organizing

containers, essential, 35

countertops. *See* bathroom, organizing; kitchen, organizing; laundry room, organizing

craft room/area, organizing, 31, 177, 187
  closet, 181-182
  cupboards, 182
  doing work (Green Light), 180-187
  dresser, 182
  evaluating before (Search-light), 178-179
  ongoing projects, 183
  planning before (Spot-light), 179-180
  work surfaces, 184

craft supplies and tools, 110, 117, 123, 180-185, 187

cupboards. *See* bathroom, organizing; craft room/area, organizing; entrance,

family; laundry room, organizing; storage room, organizing
curio cabinets, 61, 65

decision-making, 36-41
desks, children's, 118
distractions, eliminating, 35-36, 228
donation container, 35
downsizing, 199, 206, 207
  adult children and, 203, 205
  doing work (Green Light), 205-206
  evaluating before (Searchlight), 200-203
  getting rid of items, 204-207
  homeowners and, 200-201, 203, 204-205
  keeping items, 205, 206
  photographing items, 205
  planning for (Spotlight), 203-205
  relocating, 201
  sorting/packing items, 206
drawers, 68, 70, 76, 77, 95, 136, 137-138
  containers in, 100, 114
  dividers in, 114
  labeling, 108, 110, 114, 141, 142
dressers. See children's bedroom, organizing; craft room/area, organizing; master bedroom, organizing
DVDs and CDs, organizing, 148, 150-153, 157

entertainment center, 149, 150-153

entrance, family, 43, 47, 53, 62
  closet, 49, 50
  cubbies, 49
  cupboards, 49
  evaluating before organizing (Searchlight), 48
  labeling hooks, 49
  organizing (Green Light), 49-50
  planning before organizing (Spotlight), 48-49
entryway, front (formal), 31, 43, 50, 53, 226
  closet, 51, 52
  evaluating before organizing (Searchlight), 51
  organizing (Green Light), 52-53
  planning before organizing (Spotlight), 51-52

fabric, storing, 185-187
family entrance. See entrance, family
family members, involving in organizing/maintaining process, 46-47, 59, 65, 131, 149, 152, 156-157, 191, 197, 213
  See also children, involving in organizing/maintaining process
family room, organizing, 31, 145, 148, 155, 157
  closet, 149, 153-154
  dishes/bowls problem, 152
  doing work (Green Light), 149-157
  evaluating before (Searchlight), 146-147
  planning before (Spotlight), 148
filing paperwork, 163

hanging file system, 50
necessary supplies/furniture, 167-168
time for, 172
  See also Lights On Filing System
fireplace mantel and hearth, 63, 156
first aid supplies, 125, 130, 139, 143
front entryway. See entryway, front (formal)
front porch, organizing, 53
  doing work (Green Light), 46
  evaluating before (Searchlight), 44-45
  maintaining after, 46-47
  planning before (Spotlight), 45

Game Savers™ boxes, 116, 154
garage, 31
goal setting, home organization, 20, 229
  See also Spotlight organizing step
Green Light organizing step, 11, 14, 20-27, 34-36, 41, 226, 228

hampers. See laundry room, organizing; master bedroom, organizing
hard-core storage space, 25, 222, 228
holiday decorations. See seasonal/holiday items

junk drawer, 68, 70, 83-84, 87

key rack, 50

kitchen, organizing, 67
    container lids, 68, 70
    countertops, 68, 70, 84-85,
        86
    cupboards, 72-73, 75-76,
        78-81
    dishes/bowls, 68, 70, 73, 75
    doing work (Green Light),
        71-73, 75-86
    evaluating before (Search-
        light), 68-70
    glasses/cups, 72-73
    maintaining after, 86-87
    pantry, 70, 80, 81-83, 87
    planning before (Spot-
        light), 70-71
    pots and pans, 69, 78-79
    refrigerator and freezer,
        68, 70, 74, 85-86, 119
    small appliances, 69, 79-
        81, 87
    under sink, 71
    utensils, 68, 70, 76-78
knickknacks, 209
    getting rid of, 61, 63, 100,
        154
    See also curio cabinets;
        family room; organiz-
        ing

laundry basket, 113
laundry room, organizing, 189
    countertops, 191, 195, 197
    cupboards, 191, 193-195,
        197
    doing work (Green Light),
        191-197
    evaluating before (Search-
        light), 190-191
    folding laundry and, 196
    hamper, 191, 193, 194, 195
    ironing and, 197
    maintaining after, 197

planning before (Spot-
        light), 191
    premium spaces, 194-195
    putting away laundry and,
        196
    secondary spaces, 195
    semi-storage, 195
Lights On Filing System, 168-
    174, 175
Lights On Organizing System,
    11, 14, 27, 31
linen closets, organizing, 125
    doing work (Green Light),
        127-130
    evaluating before (Search-
        light), 126
    maintaining after, 130-131
    planning before (Spot-
        light), 126
living room, organizing, 55
    doing work (Green Light),
        60-64
    evaluating before (Search-
        light), 56-57
    maintaining after, 65
    planning before (Spot-
        light), 57, 59

magazine racks, 148, 157
magazines, organizing/man-
    aging, 61, 141
    See also baskets; magazine
        racks
mail, 162, 163-166, 175
    4-D plan of action, 164-166
    home office, 62
    junk mail, 163-164, 175
    kitchen, 85, 86
    shredding, 50
    sorting, 47, 164, 175
    See also paperwork, orga-
        nizing
master bedroom, organizing,

32, 89
    closet, 90, 92-93, 94-100,
        103
    doing work (Green Light),
        93-103
    dresser, 90, 92, 93, 94, 100,
        103
    evaluating before (Search-
        light), 90-92
    hamper, 95
    maintaining after, 103
    planning before (Spot-
        light), 92-93
medications, 125, 130, 131,
    139-140, 143
medicine cabinet, 136, 139-
    140, 143
memorabilia/family keep-
    sakes, 209-215
    displaying, 213
    getting rid of, 37, 39, 61,
        102, 212, 213
    Green Light organizing
        step, 213-215
    organizing tool kit, 214
    Searchlight organizing
        step, 210-211
    Spotlight organizing step,
        211-213
    storing, 213

office, home, 31, 36, 163,
    174-175

pantry. See kitchen, organiz-
    ing
paperwork, organizing, 159,
    175
    disposing of during, 170,
        173, 175
    doing work (Green Light),
        163-175
    evaluating before (Search-

light), 160-161
loose papers, 163, 166-167
planning before (Spotlight), 162-163
scanning into computer, 175
shredding personal/financial papers, 173
photographs, organizing, 213, 215
pillows, 64, 128, 129
premium space, 24, 83, 84, 222, 228

recycling container, 35, 112, 150, 155, 221
remote controls, 149, 155

school papers/awards/photos, 62, 120-122
school supplies, 117
Searchlight organizing step, 11, 14, 16-18, 27, 31, 33, 41, 226
seasonal/holiday items removing, 46, 57
short-term storage, 57
secondary space, 24, 102, 222, 228
semi-storage space, 24-25, 57, 61, 222, 228
sheets and bed linens, 93, 102, 125, 126, 128-129, 131
shelves
built-in, 62
craft room/area, 180, 181
expandable, 71
family entrance, 49
kitchen, 71, 77, 78
laundry room, 191, 193, 197
linen closet, 125
living room, 62

removable, 77
step, 77
storage room, 220, 221-222
wall, 78
shoe organizers
for bathroom items, 135, 141
for toys and games, 116
shoes, organizing
children's bedroom closet, 112
front (formal) entryway, 52, 53
getting rid of shoes, 95
master bedroom closet, 95, 103
shredder, 50, 163
spaces, categories of, 24-25
Spotlight organizing step, 11, 14, 19-23, 27, 33-34, 41, 226
storage room, organizing, 31, 32, 217, 220
cupboards, 221-222
doing work (Green Light), 221-223
evaluating before (Searchlight), 219
maintaining after, 223
planning before (Spotlight), 220

table linens, 128, 130, 131
tables and tabletops, 62-64
family entrance, 49
family room, 150, 155
front (formal) entryway, 52, 53
game tables, 150, 156-157
nightstands, 90, 92-94, 101, 103
time limits, organizing, 24, 25
tool kit, organizing, 22-23, 24, 36

toys/games/puzzles, organizing, 59, 62, 65
containers and baskets, 59, 65, 110, 113, 114, 115-117, 123, 148
donating used, 62, 115, 116, 123, 148
electronic games, 150, 152, 157
games and puzzles, 115-116, 117, 154, 157
stuffed animals, 115, 116
toy boxes, 117, 149, 155
toys, 115-116, 143
trash/waste receptacles, 50, 70, 87, 164
trash container for organizing, 35, 112, 150, 155, 221
treasures, children's, 121-122, 111

wattage scale, Lights On Organizing System, 13, 15, 31
working from inside out, 23, 34, 60, 63, 72, 90, 94, 149, 181, 221, 228

Books of Interest

ORGANIZE NOW!

This book offers practical, action-oriented advice that teaches you how to organize any part of your life in less than one week. Quick, easy-to-follow checklists let you spend more time organizing and less time reading—a perfect fit for your busy lifestyle!

ISBN-13: 978-1-60061-108-7; ISBN-10: 1-60061-108-7; hardcover with concealed spiral, 240 pages, #Z2100

NO-HASSLE HOUSECLEANING

Create a healthy, clean, and serene home with less time and effort. You'll find in-depth chapters to help you quickly and effectively clean each room in the house plus tackle laundry, stain removal, and cleaning for pet owners. There also are recipes for natural, homemade cleaning products and code-red cleaning tips for quick tidy ups.

ISBN-13: 978-1-55870-881-5; ISBN-10: 1-55870-881-2; paperback, 208 pages, #Z3754

ABSOLUTELY ORGANIZED: A MOM'S GUIDE TO A NO-STRESS SCHEDULE AND A CLUTTER-FREE HOME

Perfect for moms with busy schedules, this book offers essential organizing and scheduling advice. From organizing paperwork and children's memorabilia to completely over-hauling the home, *Absolutely Organized* has it all.

ISBN-13: 978-1-58180-955-8; ISBN-10: 1-58180-955-7; paperback, 192 pages, #Z0665

These books and other fine F+W Media titles are available at your local bookstore or from online suppliers.